# What people are saying about

## Laid

T0167489

Provocative, bold, paradigm-_        _,        _r.
This book challenges the status quo of how companies are
set up and scaled and proposes a radical alternative. I would
recommend that anyone who is serious about wanting to
make a change in their business reads this with an open mind
... and a notebook!
**Sháá Wasmund, MBE**, author of bestselling *Stop Talking, Start
Doing* and *Do Less, Get More*

*Laid Bare* moves the modern leadership and sustainable
conversation forwards, in a way few would expect, and none
will forget. Kicks the Patriarchy in the balls.
**Sam Conniff Allende**, author of *Be More Pirate*

Fantastic fun – a refreshing take on an eternal problem!
**Bruce Daisley**, author of *The Joy of Work: 30 Ways to Fix Your
Work Culture and Fall in Love with Your Job Again*

At MakeLoveNotPorn we're socializing sex, with one of many
intended socially beneficial outcomes being normalizing sex work
to be as accepted a career choice as doctor, lawyer, accountant. So
I'm delighted that Paulina Tenner has translated her experience
as a stripper into a very different kind of business book. This
refreshingly honest guide is for every entrepreneur and business
person who welcomes a completely fresh perspective on building
a company, and is full of innovative ideas, including the concept
of self-set pay, that many businesses can benefit from.
**Cindy Gallop**, Founder & CEO, MakeLoveNotPorn

Paulina is at the forefront of the new world of work. *Laid Bare* is the book all entrepreneurs need to read now.
**Paul Armstrong**, *Forbes* contributor

Make no mistake, this is a book about business. Exploring the ideas of radical transparency and self-determinism of a company going from infancy to adolescence, Tenner shows, with experience rather than presupposition, how alternative management styles can create a better place to work, improve employee performance and retention, and provide better outcomes for founders. Tenner's moonlighting as a stripper and CEO make for lively reading, taking you on her journey of self-discovery, and draws analogies seldom seen in business books.
**Chris Muktar**

In her debut book, *Laid Bare; what the stripper the Business leader learnt from the stripper*, Tenner explores disruptive cultures from "the entrepreneurship marathon" to the values of "Nude". A book perfect for a post Covid, post-truth world trying to grapple with the balance between humanity and technology - I imagine if Freud, Madonna, and Jeff Bezos gave birth to a book this would possibly be it.
**Anna Downey**

Forget about management books that sell you a formula and present a perfect case study – *Laid Bare* contains deep reflections and valuable lessons about leadership and 21st-century organizations, mixed with heartfelt and fun stories about stripping.

As Paulina shares her insights, struggles, and adventures as both a burlesque artist and businesswoman, you will find valuable lessons about both business and life. She shows the messy reality of finding a way with ideas as Teal Organisations, Holacracy, and Self-set pay, while simultaneously reflecting with depth and candour on what it personally takes to be a good leader.

Touching on a wide variety of topics such as Carl Jung's shadow work, our inner voices, Eros, Feminine Leadership, Paulina blends them masterfully together as she shares her experiences containing valuable lessons about both business and life.

**Mark Marijnissen**

Once in a while you'll have a real encounter in your life. You know they are rare. Such an encounter can be in real life, it can be a book, i feel honored to have had both experiences, to meet the audacity, vision and inner strength of this young business leader Paulina Sygulska Tenner capable to see 'beyond' that makes you believe the future will be luminous if more people dare to transgress the boundaries of their life and vision on business, leadership and life in general. A story of vitality that can inspire the next business leaders out there, laying the seeds for the new world, a 'humane' world giving space to both female and male energy present in every single person.

**Sabine Allaeys**

In Paulina's words: we live in a world on the brink of vast and important changes, where our short-sighted obsession with productivity and output has superseded intuition, receptivity and creativity. And as such, an expanded new perspective is desperately needed. Against this backdrop, what she shares - which is pretty much everything - does not disappoint. Paulina is a one off, a provocateur, an eccentric, a force of nature and also a brilliant businesswoman and innovator. Her book *Laid Bare: what the business leader learnt from the stripper* provides a unique perspective on life and on business. And on their multiple intersections for someone with huge entrepreneurial talent, guts and character, and boundless curiosity. Paula combines the emotional and spiritual with the intellectual. In addition to a book rich in stories and insights, it is fascinating to learn about her quest for self-knowledge and mastery. She provides a frank account of her ongoing dissection and exploration of who she is in her various roles, in her masculine and feminine selves, and with more or less clothes on. I've been a long standing admirer of her and of GrantTree, now I'm convinced we need to be working much more closely with her!

**Michael Solomon**

I have never read a book that brings stripping, BDSM and entrepreneurship together. Word after word, Paulina tells you exactly what you need to let happen if you are ready to take your life and business acumen to the next level of vulnerability, feminine integration and power. It inspires you to sit with the painful moments in life and business to gain real depth of who you can be, naked or in a business suit.

**Annik Petrou**

At first glance, the worlds of business and of burlesque stripping don't have a lot of similarities. But in a very neat way, these two threads in the author's life are woven together, and in the result that is laid out vividly upon the pages of this book, a unique pattern emerges where these two worlds meet and enrich each other.

In *Laid Bare: what the business leader learnt from the stripper*, by her own example of being a showgirl in her spare time and a leader using sexually explicit terms in the work context, Paulina Tenner successfully challenges the notion of NSFW [not suitable for work] and the culture of rigid professional personas, which is so pervasive in a bleak business world that has lost touch with human nature, with joy and with sensual liveliness.

**Esbensen F. R. E.**

Paulina's approach to life and business is incredibly refreshing. Here is a woman not afraid to try out new things, no matter how controversial they are, and then share her lessons learnt with others. It is very rare that you get this level of honesty and self-insight among entrepreneurs. The book is surprising and entertaining to read, it makes you turn pages as you are curious what next crazy thing is coming next!
**Monika Radclyffe**

Paulina is a fearless, passionate leader. This book is an entertaining, insightful, practical, eye opening guide for entrepreneurs and business owners today, but the lessons shared are timeless wisdom.
**Chantal Burns**, Bestselling author of *Instant Motivation* & Founder of Conscious Leadership School

With so many people writing dry books about starting a company and entrepreneurship, it is such a refreshing change to read this slightly cheeky (pun intended) parallel story from Paulina Tenner. Comparing and contrasting her personal journey as both a burlesque performer and an entrepreneur (and now investor), I loved the spirit of mischief evident in this book. In many ways starting a company is directly comparable to baring yourself. You stand in front of strangers and hope you can handle the response. Tenner's approach to "management" is also refreshing, more consensual - reminiscent of Ricardo Semler's "Maverick". An entertaining and informative journey.
**Stuart Hillston**, Psychotherapist to Entrepreneurs

Never before has business sounded as sexy as it does in Paulina's intriguing first book *Laid Bare*! The comparisons between the world of the stripper and a new start-up give a fresh take on the business world, whilst offering tantalising titbits from a performers alter-ego.

But don't let this light-hearted and playful side of Paulina's character fool you, behind the burlesque starlet there lies an intelligent businesswoman with more than a few pearls of wisdom to share with you about leadership, overcoming adversity and reaching for success. A truly fascinating read!
**Rachael 'Ginger' Butler**

*Laid Bare* is a fresh approach, bringing awareness and passionate spirit into business, replacing soul draining exploitative "work" with transparent and cooperative systems to obtain results for our benefit. From burlesque to boardroom, should we not all be dancing for joy and success?

In an era of widespread corporate greed, social injustice, and environmental destruction, Paulina brings caring, effective and creative approaches to entrepreneurship, merging the best of female and male energy, letting our most powerful passions create business and societal success.
**Dr. N. Kanungo** M.D.,C.M., FRCP(c), B.Eng. (Mech.), Life Coach.

How many times do we encounter a businessperson revealing their path, completely transparent and brutally self-critical? Paulina reveals her deep thinking and self-observation in the process of tinkering her thoughts around how to build a business (and along with it, herself) which is a rare occurrence in today's world.

It makes also something else clear. To be a successful entrepreneur, one who is different and is trying to think outside the box for the good of its people, you do have to be bold, different, determined, intelligent and have stamina of body and mind.
**Dasha M. Webb-Benjamin**, author of *Don't Chase Love - Cut to the Chase*

This is an interesting book. Paulina is refreshingly direct, and her ideas are more provocative than the stripping analogies –

though the stripping stories are interesting and relevant to the points she is making. Ideas like distributing power throughout an organisation, allowing staff to set their own salaries, and balancing the feminine and masculine qualities of leadership are all well-argued and based on thorough research as well as her extensive business experience. So peel back the covers and enjoy what she reveals!

**Chalky White**

In *Laid Bare*, Paulina reminds us that we come as multiple complex beings with a serious capacity to make the best out of our lives. If we want it. And… if we shed some unnecessary skin layers. This book, packed with delicious stripping and insightful business stories closely intertwined, is an invitation to blur my serious and burlesque boundaries. I am also taking away this affirmation: "Trusting the Universe doesn't have to be a bad approach, as long as you also realise that part of that Universe is also your very mind and your ability to be smart and decisive and committed."

**Servane Mouazan**

Brutally honest, funny, and nails down what it means to be an entrepreneur. Insightful without being dogmatic. It is loaded with well-researched alternative approaches to business and life in general. A call for a new paradigm from a business writer with a heart and a sharp mind to boot. It is for someone who believes in people and the power of the individual. Unlike with many other success accounts you truly get the feeling that nothing is omitted for a neater narrative. There is no other layer to be stripped back. A must read for business founders at all stages.

**Vaida Filmanaviciute**

This is not the typical business book you would pick up. It's forward thinking and female empowering. Raw, honest,

informative and written with humour. Easy and enjoyable to read!
**Rut Rehnstrom**

Paulina has such a unique insight into the business world which has been gifted to her from the unique journey she's been on. A highly recommended read for any entrepreneur with an open mind who is open to change. A real breath of fresh air.
**Ste Bergin**

As a former employee of Pow's it's been wonderful to read about her journey to becoming the successful female startup entrepreneur that she is today. I feel that those on a similar journey will benefit from the empowering messages and insights Pow offers throughout. It's rare to read about female leadership in a business context, reading about her perspective on it in her book is something I found to be powerful and important for today's world of work.
**Vwede Okorefe**

A modern and realistic look at business with numerous examples based on the author's experience. This book is a great source of information for those who are planning to start a business or those who want to navigate in a different direction. If you are planning to run or already own a startup this book is definitely a must read.

Difficult subjects are simply explained using metaphors of the author's experience such as her experience as a stripper which makes this book easy to understand.

I have read many business books in my life but this one now sits firmly on the "going back to" shelf especially in this time of constant flux.
**Paulina Marczykiewicz**

A very honest, heart-warming read that tells you the story of Paulina's company's journey from inception to the vibrant 50 employee, £4m turnover business it is today.

Nothing is held back, all her hopes, dreams and aspirations are laid bare for all to hear about along with glimpses of other parts of her anatomy that sound delightful. Saucy but nice, as they say, and absolutely no offence taken.

One moment I was laughing out loud at some of her more risqué characters and next minute I was shocked into silence by the brutality and helplessness of people she mentions.

The book certainly grabbed my attention and made me want to follow the growth of GrantTree, willing it to succeed and flourish every step of the way.

**Anne Anderson**

# Laid Bare

What the Business Leader Learnt From
the Stripper

# Laid Bare

What the Business Leader Learnt From
the Stripper

Paulina Tenner

BOOKS

Winchester, UK
Washington, USA

JOHN HUNT PUBLISHING

First published by O-Books, 2021
O-Books is an imprint of John Hunt Publishing Ltd., 3 East St., Alresford,
Hampshire SO24 9EE, UK
office@jhpbooks.com
www.johnhuntpublishing.com
www.o-books.com

For distributor details and how to order please visit the 'Ordering' section on our website.

ISBN: 978 1 78904 579 6
978 1 78904 580 2 (ebook)
Library of Congress Control Number: 2020936379

A CIP catalogue record for this book is available from the British Library.

Design: Stuart Davies

UK: Printed and bound by CPI Group (UK) Ltd, Croydon, CR0 4YY
Printed in North America by CPI GPS partners

We operate a distinctive and ethical publishing philosophy in
all areas of our business, from our global network of authors to
production and worldwide distribution.

# Contents

To Freya and Bob, my inner feminine and masculine characters (and a marriage of expansion and pragmatism), and to Feardinand the Great, the voice of fear. Thank you all for showing up frequently in the process of writing this.

Also, to my dad Roman for being the first example of grounded masculine in my life, and for giving Bob a lot to aspire to.

# Foreword

Yes, I used to be a stripper. Or a showgirl, more precisely, as I stripped only on stage and chose what I revealed and when. I became one about two years into running my startup, when I was so exhausted and disillusioned by being immersed in the world of business 24/7 I desperately needed a creative outlet – the more outrageous, the better. During one of my lowest points, I remember walking from Piccadilly Circus towards Charing Cross in London (most likely to another business meeting) and getting a glimpse of a fabulous burlesque show rehearsal through the door of Café de Paris, a well known cabaret establishment, which I passed on my way. Suddenly and with piercing clarity I knew: I needed to become a stripper myself. That was the answer to my desperate ache for more creativity, rebellion and juice in my life as a businesswoman. I found out, that very day, about burlesque courses in London and signed up for one with The Cheek Of It, started by Zoe Charles, a dear friend these days. I performed on various stages for about two years and even though I retired as a showgirl, the radical stripper character, the unstoppable rebel and the feminine goddess all live within me and evolve further, the more I get to know myself.

Being a stripper taught me more lessons than I could possibly imagine, a lot of which I've been able to apply to my business life. It also fed into my development as a leader. It helped me reclaim a different way of relating with my feminine part and therefore a different way of being and acting in the world. I became more open-minded and, at the same time, more whole as an individual.

In the following pages, I'd like to show you exactly how I built a company which feeds into a new paradigm and then to invite you on an exciting journey of exploring your own leadership. My inner stripper will be our chaperone, weaving in stories and

1

metaphors from the glamorous world of burlesque.

This book is for entrepreneurs, creatives, thinkers and adventurers of the future. Does "doing work" and "going to work" need to be merely a tedious necessity allowing us to do more pleasurable and interesting things in life? I'm absolutely convinced we're on the brink of a workplace revolution, and the signs of the change coming are everywhere.

Sadly, a lot of workplaces are still structured like Ford's factories at the turn of the 20th century even though our collective consciousness has very much evolved. No wonder our careers and working lives are increasingly dissatisfying. The way I see it, no mysterious, powerful "others" are to blame. Each of us can be the change and a lot of us are called to be. We must give ourselves permission to overcome conditioning, to think and act differently. This book is here to support you in this very individual process.

I don't want to underestimate the influence of global business leaders, corporation shareholders, governments. But every single one of the people who form these bodies is on their personal journey too. And it will take time, and a lot of courage, for their individual change in thinking to trickle down the vast organisations they have influence over. In the meantime, you and I can complain about how distorted the world has become, or focus on what's true and attractive to us, in this moment, and move towards that.

I believe that self-aware individuals, startups and small organisations are the incubators of social change. Because of this, I've worked in small companies and created ones pretty much all my working life, striving to remain aligned with where I believe workplaces are headed. Every now and then, when I take a breath and look up from the daily hustle, I get glimpses of what the future holds. I see a world where we choose to work, instead of having to work, because it's a fundamental expression of who we are. I see workplaces which hold space for you to discover yourself, hone in on your mastery, face your weakness and find your true path, rather than being a place where you earn enough money to (hopefully, one day) do all of the above elsewhere. I see a world where following your true path is profitable and comes without a struggle to survive in the material world on one hand, or vast compromises on the other.

That's what the future holds. Let's go there together.

# Part One

## The Naked Truth About Building A Transparent Business

# Reclaiming The Goddess

This book didn't come from the masculine, goal-oriented part of me, but from the feminine part playfully weaving her web of stories. While writing, I've had the eerie, comforting, feeling that this book existed in its finished form already, before I began. Sometimes I paused and waited for another phrase or sentence to come; I only needed to listen, knowing it was available if I tuned in carefully enough.

Based on author and teacher Michelle Cross and according to tantric teachings, the masculine energy also described as yang or Shiva represents that which is strong, steady, solid, constant, directional, active and dense. The feminine energy, yin or Shakti, is fluid, flowing, changeable, liquid, resting, vast, timeless and eternal. So where masculine is all about the left brain and the doing, the feminine is about the right brain and the being. Where yang is assertive and striving, yin is receptive and becoming. Shiva drives forward and penetrates, Shakti surrenders and receives, and in this way a balanced universe is their co-creation, their dance and their lovemaking. If either of the energies is dominant for too long, an imbalance occurs.

In the world of business, more and more founders are running their organisations from a place where the two principles meet. There's attunement to the bigger picture, often with the full surrender to the fact that its true complexity is impossible to fathom. Profit no longer comes at all costs, for there are things that matter more than how much we'll make this year and whether shareholder value increases as a result. For example, how our people feel about their work, and how they feel in general because of the work that they do. How it influences their lives and allows them to, in turn, influence the world around them. Is working in my company something that makes their lives, overall, better and more fulfilling. Do they have enough money to pay their mortgages but also enough motivation and freedom, nurtured where they work, to live fuller lives, and meet their potential and desires on a deeper level.

Minding the bigger picture is also, and quite simply, about making a tangible change in a given industry, and on the planet as a consequence. Are the human population, and other inhabitants of this world, generally better off because my company exists? It's about holding this question gently, knowing that not even the most advanced statistics and measurements can – or should be able to – put my mind at ease.

Lastly, putting aside the face value of what we deliver, how do we do what we do? Does the process, the journey towards, matter just as much as the outcome? Could the process itself be an even higher art, and a higher expression of purposefulness than reaching whatever goal we were aiming to achieve?

# The Big Reveal

Dita Von Teese, the American starlet dubbed "Queen of Burlesque" who "put the tease back into striptease", had humble beginnings. Von Teese (born Heather Sweet) was born into a working-class background and began her professional life working in a lingerie shop, decades before she could possibly afford the incredible designer underwear she later sported while bathing in a giant martini glass — just one of her many world-famous acts. This reminds me of a friend with a stage name of Princess Betty North who created a hilarious act around her working-class background. Betty, dressed from head to toe in pink lacy and satiny fluffiness, explains with heavy Northern accent what a bloke might get for getting her a pint (one pink glove off), a burger at a local joint (here the corset comes off, but stockings and underwear remain), or a full wine-and-dine experience in the poshest part of Bradford (here she proceeds with the sauciest and funniest dance accompanied by nearly full strippage).

Likewise, my own beginnings as an entrepreneurial hustler were also pretty meagre. I arrived in London in late 2006 to study at University College London as an affiliate student under the Erasmus scholarship and university exchange programme. I was thrilled as I also saw this as an opportunity to reinvent myself in a major way. I had a BA in theatre studies from Jagiellonian University in Kraków, Poland, a string of successes as a kind of student who is usually the best at everything, and also a few years' legacy of well-hidden depression and eating disorders. The cycle of relatively sophisticated (and not very obvious) self-destruction I had been stuck in proved exhausting and I was ready for a change. It was the perfect time to recreate myself.

At first I dreamt about a career in the advertising industry, but soon enough I ditched those dreams in favour of my fascination with the startup folk. I admired their audacity, the stunning nature of their arrogance expressed in a flamboyant belief that they can actually change something – in the world, in their industry, in a specific niche. I couldn't believe what these people were made of and I felt pure fascination. All of a sudden I wanted to drink beer and munch on pizza at various meetups with them (Rule no 1 of early stage founders: Thou shalt not disregard free food and alcohol). I was even willing to pretend I knew what "product-market fit" meant so I could get into some conversations. And so I did.

Before I knew it, I was one of them. It had to be. Not so much because of the free pizza, but because of the audacious and fearless spirit that warmed my heart. "I want to do something genuinely new in my industry and I know I've got, statistically speaking, maybe a 10% chance I'll make it past the first year. So what?! Of course I'm in." I was definitely hooked.

My first attempts at creating a company that actually worked commercially were rather pathetic, which tends to be the case with most founders. The business model changed every two weeks; there were grand visions but little follow-through. I felt important though: I was a co-founder now! And I felt terrible at the same time as I realised most of the meetup conversations I was previously fascinated by boiled down to a bunch of folks trying to drown their fears and struggles in the company of like-minded individuals, while often being unable to talk openly about their fears and struggles. "It's going great, this is the next big thing! I can tell you in more detail if you sign an NDA." "We have so many new sign-ups, it looks like a hockey stick – up and to the right!" "Investors are literally biting our hands off, there's so much interest." A lot of startup people I admired were as confused as I was and really struggling while trying to make their little ventures work. Those who weren't struggling, for the most part, weren't there. They were busy doing precisely the things that needed to be done. And I, for one, at least back then, had no idea what these things were.

At some point my level of frustration with myself, and the venture I was trying to push relying on zero skills and experience and a tonne of determination, reached a sufficient level that a change became necessary. GrantTree was born out of a relatively reluctant, at first, partnership with my boyfriend of a year who had just failed with his previous startup, was completely skint and, momentarily, lost his belief in his entrepreneurial career. He'd reduced his pay drastically since leaving Accenture to pursue the dreamland of the startup life and was now living in a room so small, it had no space for a desk so he literally worked from bed, or from a guest room of his close friend (who was also the MD of the company), transformed into a tiny office.

When the startup eventually closed down abruptly, the same friend, now based elsewhere, kindly allowed us to live in his apartment on credit, while we were barely making ends meet. In these jolly circumstances we started GrantTree, an advisory company in financial services set out to help innovating organisations secure Research & Development Tax Credits and R&D grants, which we do to this very day. It's just that by now, as I'm writing this, we've secured more than £140m worth of equity-free funding for our clients and live in a beautiful flat of our own in Hoxton. Back when I first got down to selling our services though, they were backed up by non-existent track record, no testimonials and no known brand. Being the relentless and never-taking-a-no-for-an-answer "saleswoman from hell", as a colleague jokingly called me much later, I got on with it, though, and started getting interest pretty much right away. And so one evening Daniel and I decided we urgently needed a company name, a website and a bank account.

If I hadn't persisted back then, pretty much against all odds, a blooming – and pretty much self-managing – company of over 40 people with strong values and four million Sterling turnover (at the time of writing) wouldn't exist today. So if a venture or a project of yours hasn't been successful, by no means does it transpire that your entrepreneurial career is over. Entrepreneurship is a marathon, with high-paced stretches, breaks and even falls included. If you feel called to create things, never give up just because a particular project failed. Treat it as useful feedback from the market and move on.

# Getting Set Up

A stripper with a "swell set-up" is one with a fab figure, making it easy to look stunning in a wide variety of get-ups and outfits. Sometimes, an act can involve taking off several layers of clothing where one outfit under another is revealed (in one of my acts I reveal three different sets of clothes as I play three characters in one act before I actually strip!). Because of this a swell set-up is a good thing though under no circumstances does it mean a size 0. Most successful "headline honeys" are often busty and beautifully curvaceous even if few of us can boast a 22-inch Dita Von Teese waist (I can't!). At the same time, being of a different body type than a typical burlesque bombshell can definitely be turned into an advantage, which I have experienced myself with my small-busted athletic figure.

The same goes for entrepreneurship or building a brand in business – not being afraid to stick out from the crowd really counts. I would go as far as to say that startups that survive have found a way of standing out and being noticed and remembered by their audience, and their supporters. This kind of courage goes hand in hand with being a true innovator or disruptor in a given industry. Some companies can create enough of a storm around their product or activity that a whole market suddenly appears, seemingly out of nowhere. Such was the case for Red Bull who created a market for energy drinks in Europe; when they first entered, the closest comparable product was coffee or perhaps Coke. The market existed in Asia (e.g. in Thailand) but an energy drink was a completely new concept in Europe. Cleverly using a network of influencers mostly in student communities (which included delivering whole boxes of the product to student parties to popularise using the drink as an alcohol mixer), they created a market which is now booming, with numerous new entrants.

As far as GrantTree goes, we knew quite early on we were going to be far from a standard corporate set-up. Creating a workplace similar to those we had escaped was not an option for Daniel or me. In the meantime, as months and then years passed, survival challenges (how the hell do we get the next £10k sale in?!) became structural challenges, where we needed to ask ourselves how to prioritise all the things we had going on. Also, how do we work together and not kill one another? Finally, more philosophical challenges emerged when we started wondering if and how we can influence the industry in which we operate. Would anyone really be worse off if we didn't exist? Why?

The team grew – from two to three, from three to ten. I was terrified to let anyone else do any work initially. I was quite convinced it would ruin everything. As luck would have it, it didn't. Instead, existing clients were better looked after as I was continually hunting for new ones and Daniel was juggling more accounts than he could handle even with seven-day working weeks. I will never forget my meeting with a guy my age we were about to bring on the team as first full-time employee. He used to work for a big bank beforehand, and took home more than three times as much as we were offering him as a starting salary (we couldn't afford more and so we advertised for a junior account exec; he was far from junior but he genuinely wanted the job). I asked our first hire-to-be what motivated him to work in a super early stage venture started by a crazy couple (with all the challenges that come with it). He said something along the lines of "I don't want to have to tell my grandchildren I worked in a bank all my life". This, coupled with the risk he was consciously taking, really moved me.

The three of us worked together happily ever after (well, for three years...). Our first employee was delighted he didn't have to be in the office by 9.00am latest and was welcome to wear "rainbow puke" clothes that he liked, instead of a shirt and tie. He was just what we needed despite much advice we received from friends and business contacts who believed we would come to regret bringing in a team member from the corporate world. Mind you, some of these people had told us that starting a business together as a couple was the worst idea possible, that we would come to split up three months or so after incorporation and they would need to decide whether to remain friends with Daniel or with me.

As the team grew (fortunately, subsequent hires felt a little less terrifying to me), questions about how to structure our work became more and more relevant. I remember a day when a business coach we were consulting with at the time, used to traditional corporate environments and frameworks, drew a future "org chart" of GrantTree on a whiteboard for us. Our hearts grew heavy, even though we didn't show it in the meeting. It didn't feel appropriate – but what else were we hoping for? What else was there to aim for? Looking back, I remember I was too overwhelmed to consider the validity of other options, also given the fact the business was now growing rapidly and I was pouring blood, sweat and tears into convincing new clients to work with our little startup every day. (I spent the weekends in a black hole of a complete emotional crash and exhaustion – I won't ever impose this kind of work pressure on myself, or anyone else, again.)

Fortunately, my co-founder had the enormous balls needed to throw everything the world was presenting to us, in terms of the possible future of our business, away. To stop and to think: "What are we building here? How is it different to the kind of workplaces we've left behind and vowed to never come back to? Is there another way?" An important part of his motivation was also to create a company that would be self-managing and wouldn't need us one day (which is true today). In this particular case, I was acting mostly from the energy I now see, from the perspective of having studied tantra and shamanism, as "distorted masculine" – progress at all costs, be it my own mental health, or even building something not actually worth building. It feels terrible to look at it this way, but it's true. Above everything else I needed to prove to myself that I was capable of creating an organisation the outer world deemed "successful". Going one level deeper, I needed to do that in order to establish a sense of safety or belonging for myself in the world – if I'm able to build a company from scratch then, clearly, I have a right to be here. I sense that a lot of founders around me act from a similar place. It's difficult for me to judge them for that, given that's exactly where I've come from. And yet, I know the world needs organisations created from a different energy, that of a wholesome masculine, which no longer needs to prove anything to himself or to the world, in union with a wholesome feminine, in order to evolve.

While I was too deep in the throes of our little company's survival battle to take a perspective, Daniel's stance was more that of a balanced or wholesome masculine – in other words logical, active, left-brain, directional. What makes sense to do? What really needs doing amongst endless things we could be doing? Where are we trying to get to by doing what we're doing?

As the team grew he put quite a lot of thought into strategy and team incentives. For some time, everyone on the team was encouraged to evaluate their own performance around goals they'd chosen for themselves. At the end of every month, they'd receive a green tick or a red cross mark on a big whiteboard in our first office (which was, in reality, a bunch of desks huddled together in the corner of our client's office, which I had miraculously secured at £500 a month). Up until one day, in a one-to-one, one of the team members told Daniel she felt like she was back in kindergarten being given gold stars on her exercise book, which makes perfect sense to me now, but didn't back then.

It started to occur to Dan and me that people who did well at GrantTree were those who were intrinsically motivated, and whose personal goals and values were aligned with those of the company. They performed well because they chose to, as a natural expression of that alignment as well as their potential, as opposed to receiving a green tick on a whiteboard.

# What Colour You Wear And How To Wear It

It doesn't take merely finishing a burlesque course to become a successful showgirl, even if that's where most of us start (I took quite a few courses with The Cheek Of It – warmly recommended!). It's easy to call yourself a professional stripper but it takes experience, brand recognition and popularity to really become one. Even though I performed across many countries (including Canada and Japan!) during the years I was an active showgirl, I never intended to pursue burlesque as my main income stream, but more as a hobby. Some of my stage colleagues did, though, and proceeded to host their own cabaret nights and even to create one-woman shows. And while new starlets kept being released into the world by a few of the burlesque schools in town, ladies such as Rubyyy Jones or Lolo Brow kept being booked, as they'd worked hard and consistently on their brands and cabaret careers.

By the same token everybody – or nearly everybody – in the startup world likes to call themselves "teal", as per colour-coded methodology introduced by Frederic Laloux in *Reinventing Organisations.* According to Laloux there are several types of organisations which reflect different stages of human consciousness. Red organisations, purely command and control based, such as mercenaries or street gangs, are less complex than amber (think armies or government agencies), which themselves are less elaborate than orange organisations. The orange paradigm is measurement-based, performance-driven and representative for how most corporations operate today. Most likely you have experience of working in an orange organisation (I do), following reporting lines and achieving KPIs in order to boost shareholder value.

Green organisations are more conscious of the people that

compose them. They tend to be consensus-driven and purpose-driven. Cooperatives or some charities tend to operate this way. At the top of the pyramid – at least when it comes to the levels of consciousness we are currently able to access and create from – are teal organisations. Those operate like a human organism, an ant colony, or, indeed, a city. This means that to an outsider such an organisation could easily look like anarchy, with no order or rules. Yet it works and, like a human body, it works really well in a wide variety of ways, some of which are easy to examine and some of which are very unobvious and way too complex to categorise using knowledge readily available to us.

In the same way that no single entity controls a city, no one is the single decision maker at the top of a teal company (though, more often than not, there will be a single vision holder, or a CEO). The power is distributed. And even though the chances are that to an uninformed observer the organisation looks chaotic, there are defined ways in which information flows and decisions are made. It's just not what we're used to with pyramid structures where there is practically no connection between those making decisions at the top, and those doing the work on the ground at the bottom of the structure. Three principles are key to teal: self-management, wholeness (or bringing one's whole self to work) and evolutionary purpose. The last one means that the purpose continually evolves according to needs and insights of people within the organisation and information coming from the market. It's not stagnant or simply dictated from above.

Importantly though, teal isn't really something you can necessarily *be*, as this stage of organisational consciousness entails constant evolution or movement. It's more something that you practise. As a stage of organisational development attuned with the highest levels of human consciousness, it escapes precise definitions, unlike the preceding stages. In a similar way, it's a challenge to understand and map exactly how a city operates. Or a human body, with all the pieces of it we've barely scratched the surface researching. And yet they do operate very successfully.

Without a doubt, there are teal practices though. Or, more accurately, practices and structures that can support a teal oriented development. In my experience, holacracy, which GrantTree adopted in early 2017, is one of them. In case you aren't familiar with the term, in short, it's a governance and operational system that presents an interesting alternative to hierarchy. I like to compare it to the lean startup methodology, which advocates staying attuned to what your market needs, making hypotheses and checking them as frequently as possible. Holacracy proposes a similar approach in the space of company governance – testing and trying new things frequently to see how they work in practice, by making the cost of change very low.

And so, in a single holacracy meeting you can implement a new policy, create a new role or amend an accountability of an existing role. The encouragement is to "be a Ferrari" and move fast. If what got implemented doesn't work, you can change it or bin it in the next governance meeting (or even asynchronously outside of a meeting, which we do using software called Holaspirit). Because this approach to governance is transparent, collaborative, and very dynamic, it offers a much better chance to reflect the actual – and ever-changing – reality of how the company operates, as opposed to defining a set of standards and trying to retrofit how the organisation functions day to day into them. The same goes for strategy and future planning – instead of those being set from above with the rest of the company playing catch-up, sometimes over months and years, strategic goals remain closely related to, and get readjusted according to, what's happening "on the ground".

In my experience, holacracy as a system is perfectly scalable and supports transparency and flow of information across the team. It supports a hierarchy of roles rather than a hierarchy of people. Anyone (for example a new joiner Tom) can quickly look up which role makes a decision on what, the accountabilities of a given role, or what's our policy on x, and so be informed how the company operates. As the reality of the business changes (as it inevitably does), roles and their accountabilities evolve, domains and particular policies change to reflect this reality more precisely. This gets immediately reflected in the company's structure.

I wouldn't describe holacracy as a step on the way to teal (as some do) but perhaps as a tool that encourages teal-like practices. Let's remember that holacracy has nothing to do with a set of particular values though, it's merely a framework that can support pretty much any system of values. As someone pointed out in a HolacracyOne (creators of holacracy) training I attended, you can use holacracy to start up a church just as effectively as to scale up a brothel. I agree. It's the ultimate structured blank page allowing you as a founder to create exactly the kind of structure

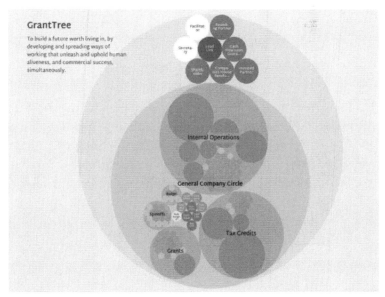

**GrantTree's current purpose and momentary company structure
reflected on Holaspirit**

(and culture, which inevitably follows structure) you need. And to continuously adapt it so it stays fit for purpose.

From what I've seen, a lot of startups and small companies who claim to "be teal" are in the midst of all-encompassing chaos (something my company most definitely lived through), where everybody tries to do whatever falls in their lap and everything – for now – somehow holds together. You may have experienced within your own company or department how people with best intentions would sometimes pull in different directions, often completely unbeknownst to each other. Perhaps you've even tried to introduce appropriate systems for things to feel more under control. Perhaps you've experienced first-hand the difficulty of trying to bring people together and help them work together smoothly, without micromanaging them.

Particularly in early startup environments more often than not randomness reigns. But teal seems to be a cool branding to stick on top of this chaos so it becomes a smooth-sounding excuse for a simple lack of structure, accountabilities, role definitions, operational clarity and/or an absence of strategy (much like "agile" eventually became abused as a slick label for what was really a total lack of structure and planning). An actual company operating in the teal space is one that, in my perspective, has not only dealt with all the above with considerable maturity, but, in a way, transcended and included those frameworks (to still fall back on them when there's a need). As opposed to never having considered how to adopt a clear operational structure out of lack of experience, laziness, or peer pressure (in some startup circles, structure at work is deeply uncool).

Is my company an expert on teal? Hardly. We're growing up, for sure, and every internal or external challenge we face gives us an opportunity to become a more mature company. I still see plenty of evidence though that we're just as good at screwing up as we are at being an example of an evolved workplace of the future. We've stayed true to what we believe, though, and to the path (much) less travelled in terms of how we operate as a commercial organisation. It's fair to say we strive to operate in a teal space as long as, in line with the above, teal isn't seen as a specific destination, but an ongoing, evolving practice. In other words, a state of union (not always of balance!) between the feminine and the masculine forces in the organisation, combining chaos with order (Dee Hock, founder of VISA, called it a "Chaordic organisation"), attunement to the present moment with dynamism and change. A sense of perspective is married to focus on the task at hand. An ability to be still when facing a challenge goes hand in hand with sharp decisiveness, when the moment calls for it.

As an example, the Head of People in my company recently had a tension to do with centralisation of power. To move power away from one important role present in every circle (the so-called Lead Link), she decided to introduce a new policy that removed the accountability of assigning roles from the Lead Link and, by doing so, further distributed power. After some feedback from people in relevant roles, the proposal got implemented and is a perfect example of how GrantTree would sometimes modify even rules encompassed within the holacracy Constitution in order to meet the needs of our culture.

In summary, teal is an interesting idea and holacracy an interesting tool to consider for any self-aware organisation. What they are not is a destination but merely a stage of evolution. They helped us create the backbone of our culture. And the way I see the nature of our culture these days is that, just like in any passionate lovemaking, sometimes Shiva (or Yang quality) is on top, sometimes Shakti (or Yin). But there is generally a similar measure of energy coming from the feminine and the masculine aspect. It's the "ecstatic union" of the two, as tantric masters would put it, or a chaordic paradigm, as business people would put it, that becomes a birthplace of ideas, practices, and systems that will transform the world as we know it today.

# F*ck Teal, Be... Nude!

I remember a season when wearing green seemed to be the thing. We got quite a few electric green GrantTree hoodies made but then people got bored of them and unexciting grey (with our green logo on the back) gained popularity again. Helpfully, they were cheaper to order. There was also a request or two for a jet-black edition, with a rainbow logo, incorporating colours of the Rainbow flag. I even remember some journalist's snarky comment on the Duchess of Cambridge's green dress (or was it a coat?) she made some sort of appearance in that "'forest green' belongs just there: in the forest".

Teal has also had its season, not just in the startup jargon. To be honest, it's still a colour I personally like to wear, it's quirky and the only version of blue I look good in, given my natural autumn colour palette. But there's something better (and quite a bit more exciting) than teal and that's... Nude! Obviously, as a showgirl you're absolutely guaranteed to get more enthusiasm sporting it. And in the world of organisational consciousness, it's time to define a new paradigm. Teal on steroids. In other words, Nude.

Nude builds on teal and as a paradigm entails complete internal transparency of information, financial and other. In other words, everything is accessible to everyone inside the company, from payroll to financial forecasts and amount of cash in company bank accounts in real time. After all, if you expect your people to handle important decisions to do with clients, culture and even the company's future, why wouldn't you give them access to all the information they can possibly have? Nude takes the belief that people are wired to do great things given enough trust and space to develop and express their mastery to its extreme. As such it's the purest form of open culture, more on this below.

For understandable reasons, Nude is too scary for most companies even to consider. A lot of leaders are terrified for those who report to them to know too much, mostly because having access to information that is only exclusively available helps them hold more power. If your company is in that position and looking to implement some principles of open culture, the priority will be to empower its people and create space where they have autonomy, can take ownership of resources they have and, because of this, let their mastery shine.

When it comes to financial transparency, I often get challenged with the argument that people who have never run businesses themselves won't be able to understand how things work and will get into sheer panic when the cash levels are low. It isn't completely groundless. Many people who work with you, or for you, indeed haven't ever set up their own business and aren't aware of the natural cycle of cashflow highs and lows. They may (understandably) be worried they won't get paid or even conclude that a temporary cashflow low means the whole business will go under. They may not understand how to read company accounts or financial reports. This is where patience and financial education is needed. In the bigger scheme of things, staff will feel empowered to be working for a Nude employer and are more likely to truly take ownership of their work.

As much as it is rewarding, the road to Nude is also marked with challenges, such as creating and sustaining the company culture that supports it.

# What The Hell Is "Company Culture"

"It's a great culture, we get free pizza on Friday afternoons!" "And we have a beer fridge, accessible all week, how about that?!" "These other guys though, they have a pink slide in the middle of their office, going from top floor to the bottom one. No one really uses it but pretty cool to have one, no?"

I don't engage in conversations about culture very often these days because they leave me frustrated. The term "company culture" has become similarly clichéd to "being agile", in other words, it can mean absolutely anything. Most likely an entirely different thing to the person you are engaging in a conversation with than it means to you. There's an expectation on an employer to be able to demonstrate a good/strong/positive company culture (or an impression of such) and so they employ their marketing machines to do so. Reality does rarely measure up to the marketing message though.

I'm more of a fan of talking about why cultures suck, because only a reality check can result in a meaningful change. Which is why, I would hereby like to give permission to people who feel a little courageous and don't like to take themselves too seriously to declare: "our culture is absolutely shit in the following ways". This is obviously completely meaningless unless I can follow through first, and so I will. At GrantTree our culture is absolutely shit if what you need is a very clear external idea of how well you do your job. It's also shit if you want for someone to tell you exactly what to do to progress your career. It's shit if taking feedback – sometimes not in the gentlest of ways – isn't your strong side. Finally, it's shit if you hate having to adjust to change frequently. You have to make decisions about things like your own pay, knowing that all your peers will get to review your thinking and the final figure. On top of this, one of the founders (yours truly) makes filthy and/or silly jokes regardless of the occasion. (I do draw a line where people could potentially be upset or offended.)

What the hell is company culture to me, then? It's a way we choose to be together in the workplace, behaviours and dynamics which are true today, as current reality and not an aspiration. I've also heard company culture described as defined by that (be it a behaviour, practice, choice) which is rewarded or being equal to how people go about getting things done in an organisation. Both are good bottom-up definitions as they imply staying in touch with what's actually occurring, rather than an aspiration of the management.

For example, I could say that our holacracy practice is well established. On the face of it, it sounds okay but is it actually true? Let's examine. Three years after we implemented holacracy as an operational and governance system we'd like to believe we have embedded it to a point, where the old dynamics (based on implicit hierarchy for example) are no longer at play. That's an aspiration, not a current reality. I could also say that one of our top priorities is to create a workplace where people are trusted, feel valued and have tools to claim their power; and that we're practically committed to this priority being upheld in everyday work. That commitment is a current reality. Whether we have a beer fridge and a "relaxed, supportive atmosphere" in the office means effectively nothing. So does "integrity" or "trust" or, my favourite bullshit bingo phrase, "commitment to client's success", written on a poster.

# Baring It All (Or: Principles Of Open Culture)

Different clubs I've worked in allow different levels of stage nudity. "Burlesque nudity" typically involves a tiny G-string or a stick-on merkin – a piece to cover up our lady garden, usually sparkly and beautifully decorated – and nipple pasties. Those can be plain or have tassels attached which spin around when boobies are shaken with the perfect technique. I have even seen a dancer wear tassels on her butt cheeks once! She had her spinning technique absolutely nailed. Some clubs allow a topless finale while others (not many) have a full nudity licence. Regardless of what the rules are, the moment of baring it all is most eagerly awaited by the punters, particularly if preceded by the perfect amount of tease (enough to whet the appetite while not being drawn out for so long your audience got frustrated or lost interest).

We've called ourselves many things throughout the years at GrantTree but one thing stuck: an open culture company. This is likely to be confusing, as the term can entail, in practice, many different things. Open cultures come in different shapes and sizes but, at least in my experience, have some common properties. Here is a shortlist I've compiled thinking through not just our story at GrantTree but companies I've interacted with and read about.

1. Rebelliousness, or conscious disagreement with the status quo.

Open cultures are created, and sustained, by men and women with balls. Unless there's conscious effort applied over time, business dynamics tend to revert to what's considered "normal" in the wider world. So what's needed in order for an open culture company to work is a rebellious spirit (often underpinned by a degree of disillusionment with the status quo) and a can-do attitude. Yes, an open culture is generally more difficult to implement – particularly at scale – than a hierarchical corporate set-up. Yes, you will likely need to make short-term profit sacrifices as you focus more on consciously building the kind of culture you want for the business to have both now and in the long-term. In essence, a pair of balls is definitely required.

2. Belief that people are fundamentally wired to do good work.

In the 1950s, scientist Douglas McGregor, while working for Massachusetts Institute of Technology's Sloan School of Management, developed his famous Theory X and Theory Y to describe work motivation and people management. According to Theory X, supervision and external rewards or penalties are required to motivate people to do any good work. According to Theory Y, job satisfaction is key, people are intrinsically motivated and generally want to better themselves without a specific reward in return. A key insight offered by McGregor was that whichever theory you believe, you are likely to find plenty of evidence in the workplace that it's correct. So it becomes extremely important to make a conscious choice about which world you think you live in. We choose to follow Theory Y. This doesn't mean external rewards (and fair pay of course!) are meaningless. They are more than likely to be important to people, in particular depending on their stage in life and the financial challenges they face. Still, the key reason why we choose to work is to be better humans.

3. Transparency of business information (financial or other).

Unhealthy power dynamics in traditional organisations are built on secrecy and selected access to information. While different open culture companies favour different levels of transparency when it comes to financial data for example (not everyone is ready to be Nude!), there's a noticeable movement towards general accessibility of business information. This reduces office politics and makes it easier to understand how and why decisions are made. At GrantTree, all business and financial information is internally available.

4. Belief that people, while not being equal, are all worthy.

We've all heard about A players and B players. A players tend to hire B players (so not to be threatened by them), who tend to hire C players and so on. Interestingly though, when a friend comes to you to complain about difficulties at work you're not likely to say, "Sadly, it seems to me that you're just a B player." I firmly believe we all can, and do, shine as long as we're in the right role, working on the right team (which is also why, in general terms, I don't believe in firing fast, another well-known corporate principle). While equality is a fallacy in the world of business (teams thrive because people have different strengths and can step into different roles, carrying various degrees of responsibility), worthiness is not. We are all worthy of being seen in our humanity, in our strengths and our struggles in exactly the same way.

# Showing Your Arse To A Wider Audience (Or: How To Scale Open Culture)

In many ways company culture, no matter how evolved, is like a stripper's arse – pretty and exciting if shown in the right light and framed by sexy or desirable objects. Of course, there are arses of seemingly impeccable quality. But if you are an owner of such an arse, only you will know how many hours of tirelessly doing squats and lunges were invested into creating it. Most of us regular bread eaters though have either hairier butt cheeks than we might like, a wee bit of cellulite or flatter arses than are considered desirable in the age of the Kardashians. One of any stripper's dilemmas that's near the top of their priority list is ensuring your arse remains attractive as it gets bigger (and some arses, believe it or not, do!). Many strippers use arse makeup to cover up blemishes or uneven skin (just foundation – eyeshadows or lipstick don't quite work in this context). Well-cut underwear is essential as it can do your arse a big favour (quite literally saving your arse!) as opposed to highlighting its shortcomings. Many strippers wear a G-string with straps of sequins (or satin, or lace) hanging around the buttocks and down the side of the upper thigh for the final reveal to showcase all the right curves. Some strippers wear barely-there nude fishnet tights which don't come off underneath stockings or other garments which do. All in all, there are quite a few tricks one can use and this chapter outlines how a company with a good culture, just like a good arse, can remain attractive as it gets bigger.

I've lost count of all the coffees and lunches I've had with people who challenged me on various aspects of open culture companies. This probably happens even more than I get asked about my stripping adventures these days! There are two things that come up most often. Challenge No 1: your company has 40 people in it, wait until it's 200 and more, and most of what you practise will have to go out of the window. Challenge No 2: most people don't want to know their colleague's salary, let alone set their own one in the knowledge of the fact everyone else will know what it is and likely have an opinion. How the hell do you find people that are prepared to go through this?

The answer that comes up in response to the first challenge is very succinct, possibly because I've come against it so many times. If you think companies must always lose their focus on values, and that they must let go of the belief that well-being can be as important as profitability as they grow: you are right. That's likely the only thing that happens in your reality, or the only thing you pay attention to, which is why you believe what you believe; it's very straightforward. If you'd like to take a sneaky peek into my reality and what I not just wish but *know* is possible, pick up a book such as *Maverick! The Success Story Behind the World's Most Unusual Workplace* by Ricardo Semler, grandfather of open culture companies (in my humble opinion), *Reinventing Organisations* by Laloux or *An Everyone Culture* by Kegan and Lahey. All of them present research and facts about large companies (a thousand and more employees) who have implemented different, fascinating and incredibly radical at times forms of open culture, and are commercially thriving. There is a variety of ways to structure a large company (dividing it into distributed, self-managing teams, for example) that allows it to maintain the dynamism, enthusiasm and values of an early-stage company. Is it easy? Not particularly, since the collective consciousness generally maintains that large companies are a necessary evil that slowly corrupts all in it, and around it. Is it doable? As demonstrated by many, without a doubt.

In connection to the second point, I feel inspired to respond more at length. We find people who are able and willing to take charge of their career progress, and their pay, with care and attention to their world and their motivations for wanting to join us. The issue is, in theory anyone could – and should be able to, possibly at some point in the future – work for GrantTree. But GrantTree isn't going to work, at its present state of organisational evolution, for everyone. We do our best to find out if it's likely to fulfil the expectations of an individual and provide a space to flourish, as opposed to an environment which is too overwhelming to be enjoyed. We do this by learning about people's way of cultivating relationships and making meaning in the world as a key part of our recruitment process. There is a particular framework we use, derived from the work of Harvard scientist Robert Kegan (and described in *A Guide to the Subject-Object Interview: Its Administration and Interpretation*) which helps us understand how much complexity a given individual is able to navigate. It's a fascinating way of looking at the evolution of consciousness post childhood, building on the work of Jean Piaget. According to Kegan, most adults are somewhere in between a stage of development he refers to as socialised, and the following one, branded as self-authoring. The first one translates to, broadly speaking, a stage in life when one's core identity isn't resilient in the face of conflicting feedback and/or challenges brought on by exposure to different environments, such as home, work life, social circuit. The behaviour or beliefs of a socialised person may differ substantially depending on the social context they are in. A self-authored individual, on the other hand, has a clear internal framework designed to make meaning of the challenges they face, and to navigate conflicting external feedback. The inner standards are strong enough to provide a thread guiding them through the labyrinth of complexity that modern life entails. This is, out of necessity, a simplification of Kegan's theory. On top of this, in many cases an individual is in one of four intermediary phases that come in between the two stages described.

Our task, when interviewing candidates as part of the open culture interview stage, is to find out whether their self-authoring system is robust enough to withstand the demands of our workplace. These include managing one's time and resources, setting one's own standards for what constitutes good work and reviewing one's performance, curating one's career in the organisation and navigating the pressures which inevitably arise in working relationships with others. All things considered, setting and reviewing one's pay probably no longer seems like such a big deal in the context of the other challenges of self-management. To conduct an interview well – and I've learnt this the hard way – is to be deeply attuned to the candidate's world and meaning-making mechanisms without identifying with them or even looking for a bridge between their world and yours, which is what many of us naturally do in social interactions with unknown people. In other words, it's an art, which I'm definitely still perfecting. I realise this especially in the context of having been masterfully interviewed by a scientist within Kegan's organisation Minds at Work to help provide more research data. To this day, meeting candidates and gaining an insight into their world through our take on the Subject-Object Interview remains one of my favourite things to do.

# Growing On The Job

A great stripper isn't a one-trick pony – she or he has many outfits, acts, personalities and stories that develop as their career progresses. In fact, a lot of earlier work is often discarded because a stripper just like an artist of any other kind might say, "This isn't me anymore." During my burlesque career I developed about ten different acts, one or two to be staged at one show only, and performed on three continents. This is likely to be one of the most fulfilling factors of a successful stripping career – it takes you places, both physically and mentally. You learn to read different audiences, just like an entrepreneur might uncover and learn different markets. You then adjust your acts according to both what's in the demand but also, and even more importantly, which parts of you you want to showcase, celebrate, or have a good laugh at.

I'm a big fan of DDOs, or Deliberately Developmental Organisations, a term coined by Kegan and Lahey in their excellent work *An Everyone Culture: Becoming a Deliberately Developmental Organisation*. There aren't enough of them in the world yet for this to be a well-known paradigm but certainly more and more are being born, started by people who believe in a new way of relating to work. Some of them don't call themselves a DDO or aren't even familiar with the term but have a very clear focus on people development as a top priority, alongside sustainability. A company called Decurion, based in Hollywood and described in the book mentioned above, takes people development so seriously that it recruits interns as young as 16 and places them in environments designed to help develop strengths and skills necessary to self-manage and grow into fully empowered professionals. These people learn to, from an early age, expect personal growth from their workplace.

Having recruited dozens of millennials at GrantTree, I

see a promising trend in connection with their work-related needs, different to the generations which came before. Because of this, ambitious organisations are now under pressure to offer environments truly supporting of wholesome personal development in order to stay competitive as workplaces. A recent conversation with a colleague who used to work for a high street bank made me smile. The bank in question effectively competes with Google and Facebook for top talent and, predictably, doesn't have a hell of a lot to offer that could help outperform these two as a recruiter. In a truly eye-watering effort to amp up the coolness factor, the corporation (when my colleague worked there) introduced dress-down Fridays where chinos were considered an appropriate outfit. As long as they were beige.

All in all, even huge, slow-moving monster companies are being forced to change, little by little. They are forced to change by those of us who refuse to subscribe to the "give everything – burn out to a crisp – give up work altogether and move to Bali" career model. And this gives me joy. Change comes from within and later manifests on the social and eventually global level. Startups and small companies are, as usual, an incubator of social change. The wheels that set everything else in motion.

# How Much Are You Worth?

Many burlesque performers, particularly when they first start up, perform for free, sometimes out of the sheer joy of showcasing their act to a new audience, sometimes because they don't quite know how to create paid-for performance opportunities or feel uncomfortable asking for money. I remember the first time I asked for £100 per act, where my starting out price used to be £50. It took courage, some experience and also a realisation of how much I've already invested into my hobby, in terms of made-to-measure costumes and obviously lots of time spent creating and rehearsing my acts, to ask for higher compensation. Once I got to about £150 (for performing two acts in a single show or the same act twice during two shows on one night) asking for more got trickier. Only performers with very well established international careers could command high fees, at least from the promoters I was working with at the time, and I knew that. I needed to get creative in terms of expanding my overall value-add and the types of services I could provide. That's when I offered to a promoter of a well-known all-night dress-up extravaganza to curate a small burlesque show which she wanted to host twice in one night as part of the many attractions her large-scale event offered. Now I not only performed but also acted as a compère of the mini show, and recruited and managed other artists being part of it. This opened up the doors to more responsibility, a wider range of services I could provide and higher earnings.

A lot of my friends are startup founders and businesspeople. Quite a few of my friends are healers, and some are strippers. I want to talk about two healer friends to demonstrate something that feels true and important to me, in the context of the marriage of the feminine and the masculine leadership in business. Healing is essentially an art of the feminine aspect or principle. It requires being deeply in tune with your client or patient, and usually with the wholeness of their being rather than just an aching shoulder, the sadness within them, or a cold that wouldn't go away. Many healers, like friend A, let's call her Anna, develop this capacity to a very high level but at a cost of the thriving of the masculine principle within them (again, regardless of their gender). Anna, a masseur and reiki practitioner, knows her price in one of the markets she could be shooting for and sticks to the lower end of it. On the surface it sort of makes sense: she remains competitive and her regular clients (like me) who recognise her value, which is quite a bit higher than what she charges, remain loyal because of this. It doesn't make sense to go elsewhere because she's fantastic and I'm honestly grateful and happy the price is low. It keeps the fear-based part of my ego ("who are you to spend so much money on yourself?") in its comfort zone.

Then, there's friend B, let's call her Betty. Betty had a strong vision during a retreat where we met that she would become a dakini or a tantric massage healer (where her services don't involve direct sexual interaction with clients). She decided she would take a top-of-the-range training she couldn't, at the time, afford, with teachers she truly admires. It so happened (coincidence or serendipity?) that one of those teachers was also in the very same retreat with us. Betty approached that teacher being transparent about her financial concerns. The teacher, to her amazement, offered to cover the course fees under Betty's promise she was going to do an apprenticeship with them after the course and work giving massages to real clients to pay the costs back. I was taken aback when she told me she was able to do that after a mere two weeks (!) of giving tantric massages priced at $500-650 per 2-3 hour slot.

There remained the cost of flights from Europe to the US where the training took place, accommodation and food during the course. This amounted to several thousands of pounds Betty had never had in her bank account all at once. Committed to her vision, she launched a crowd-funding campaign, explaining in a very inspiring way how she found her calling and precisely how she was going to follow it. On top of this, she outlined how much it would cost, and exactly what vision she had of bringing in the money from different sources (as opposed to "trusting the Universe" it would somehow turn up). I felt very comfortable to invest in this inspiring and well-put-together campaign in exchange for getting a session when she was back in London after her training and apprenticeship, even though I barely knew her at the time. (By the way, trusting the Universe doesn't have to be a bad approach, as long as you also realise that part of that Universe is also your very mind and your ability to be smart and decisive and committed. Betty did, and so all the guidance she needed arrived.)

On her return to London, Betty – a traveller, who had no accommodation here – identified several people who believed in her and happily offered for their home to be temporarily turned into a temple/sacred space where she could see donation-based clients and those, like me, who had supported her through the crowd funding campaign. She did set a suggested donation price per session (up to 3h) to £75 which is, by the way, higher than what Anna charges per hour. When I came for my session she greeted me in a space which, even though someone's flat, was perfectly set up. First, we had a conversation about where we were both at in our lives and she mentioned she was "shooting for mastery", in other words aiming to be world class at what she does, with the right amount of practice and in the right time. I absolutely and unquestionably trust that's where she is going, just six months after fully committing to her calling, simply because of her presence and energy. Our session had stunning results for me in terms of insights and inspiration. This doesn't mean she is a world-class healer right now and I had some improvement feedback for her (which she clearly asked for). But I sense she is holding point of that intention with everything that she does. At the end of the session I asked for her PayPal details so I could donate extra, regardless of the fact I had already paid for the session when I contributed to the crowd funding campaign. I believe in her and I also feel that by supporting her intention of shooting for mastery, I support my own.

Interestingly, something similar often happens, energetically, in my startup investments. I see somebody with a vision who is willing to do their utmost to make it happen. This doesn't mean waiting for stars to align and for inspiration to strike. This means showing up, every day, to work with the actual reality of the world right here and right now. When I meet people like this, to a degree it doesn't matter to me whether they'll succeed, in this current venture; maybe they'll discover the vision wasn't right, the timing wasn't right, the market wasn't ready, it doesn't matter. But I meet this level of commitment with my own level of commitment to the unravelling of human potential that can heal the planet and solve all manners of civilisational crises. In this case, this belief manifests in putting my money, as an early-stage angel investor, where my mouth is. I give you my commitment and passion, for your commitment and passion.

And, because my inner masculine has the space to show up and support the investment decision, I will definitely make a judgement on whether the business plan is sustainable and makes sense on the level of logic. Has the founder done the work to understand, as much as possible, what it takes to succeed in their market with the competitors that they have? Knowing that most startups fail, I still strive to make money on exits of some of my investments. I would like to be able to invest even more as my wealth grows (which is the plan) in line with my belief around the consequences of unravelling of human potential, as expressed above. To sum up: ideally, I invest when I feel so aligned with the founder's intention and energy that whether I make or lose money matters less. In other words, I ask myself if a given investment would still feel good looking back at it once the venture has failed. If the answer is "hell yes", I'm in.

Circling back to Anna, I wish (from the perspective of her business development) she started charging me more, sooner. Having a different strategy than Betty, these days she has a small team of masseurs working with clients across London while she is focused more on administration and less on delivery. It's just that in order for this model to be financially viable, she needs to charge more than previously so there's room for her to take commission on massages delivered by her associates. Understandably, I'm reluctant to pay more given someone else (even though trained by her) delivers the service. I do, as I'm keen to support her business, but would have felt more comfortable if a different pricing structure was in place from the start.

# On Getting Paid

Showgirls or up-and-coming cabaret artistes are typically paid little per act (back when I performed £50-£150, which may sound like a lot for a five-minute act but count travel and make-up time, costume cost, rehearsal time and you'll arrive at a conclusion it's by far not the most profitable career one could choose). However, those strippers who stand out from the crowd and develop an impeccable personal brand can sometimes command their wages according to what they feel they are really worth. I have even seen a showgirl's contract clearly stipulating she refuses to be flown to her performance location by the client with the Ryanair airline. Also, those who choose to do table dances and get really good can typically count on quite a few tokens of gratitude (read: a stack of bills) being slipped behind their suspenders. Also, they can branch out to becoming compères and hosting entire shows (like I did) or even run their own nights. There, financially speaking, the sky is the limit.

At GrantTree people are expected to determine the monetary value of the work they do on a regular basis. Establishing self-set pay in the company has been our ambition ever since Daniel and I read *Maverick!* by Ricardo Semler. These days, with roughly 40 people in the company, like not many other businesses in the world we practise full financial transparency. This means it's clear how financial decisions are made, what resources the company has, how they are deployed and exactly who is accountable for exactly what. This is supported by holacracy, which provides a framework making it easy to check what roles given people hold and what responsibilities these roles have assigned to them.

In terms of self-set pay, people regularly assess their own performance as part of a self-assessment process. This is then combined with three other sources of data: market research to assess how much they could earn elsewhere, budgeting data to assess how much the holacracy "circles" they belong to can afford, and a long-view progression self-assessment. All of these are critical pieces of information one must gather to adjust their pay upwards or even downwards. Nobody has the power to approve or disapprove a pay decision – it's the person's responsibility to integrate the substantial information (such as job market data) and the feedback they receive during the decision process, and to come to the best decision they can, rooted in their own sense of integrity. The decision process has four steps:

1) gathering information;
2) making a proposal based on that information;
3) receiving feedback on that proposal;
4) making a final decision (which may be different from the proposal).

The person making the decision about their own pay is in full and sole control of the proposal and the decision steps. They can ignore the feedback received if they choose to. Needless to say, this is quite a task, which takes maturity and courage. A lot of people, understandably, feel under a lot of pressure when making their pay decisions, which wasn't there in their past workplaces where the decision was made (and announced to them in secret) by somebody else. Still, they choose to work with us, despite the often significant challenges that this sort of workplace presents, seeing them as opportunities to grow.

Some founders I talk to get very excited about self-set pay, some are horrified by it. A lot of people ask how come every second employee doesn't decide to pay themselves a million pounds. If you make a little effort to put yourself in the shoes of someone making a pay decision in our company, it very quickly becomes obvious why. Firstly, you have access to the company accounts and it's obvious we don't have the enough cash required to pay you that kind of money and to be able to cover other costs that we have. Then, during the multi-step decision process you are required to run, you will need to justify clearly why the job you are doing for the company is indeed worth £1million. This will be challenged from all directions and some people may even feel genuinely concerned about what's going on in your life emotionally speaking, given this is a proposal you are putting forward. You can still implement the proposal, despite all the feedback; the trouble is you are also the one who needs to deal with the consequences. But perhaps the most important factor is simply that people simply don't want to be paid an unfairly large amount of money that they don't deserve. If you recall our earlier discussion of Theory X and Y, this is part of the Theory Y perspective: people actually want to do the right thing, and the self-set pay process is designed to support them in doing that, rather than futilely try to stop them from deliberately breaking everything (which, we both assert and observe, they do not want to).

I've also been asked what impact people being encouraged to regularly review their pay has on the bottom line. Is it sustainable for the company? My answer typically is that if it weren't sustainable to pay our people fairly, we should be considering changing our business model. I also don't believe that our wage bill is necessarily higher than those of companies in our sector and of equivalent size. The disparities between higher and lower paid people are simply much less significant. Also, there are no special deals or bonuses given to those who are good at befriending the boss and/or arguing their case.

Does people's pay ever get adjusted downwards? Not often but it has happened a couple of times when an employee changed their remuneration as a result of a role change in the company, for example migrating to a different department and taking on a role that's valued lower in the marketplace. The same process needed to be followed to make sure the new, lower pay was a fair one.

All in all, I think we are doing a relatively good job to appreciate the vastness of cultural stories money is tied up with and how it represents entirely different things to different people. For many, the amount of money they earn is a measure of worthiness, also in comparison to peers. For others it's tied to a sense of security and being able to have the life they want (which seems appropriate on the face value until you realise how many other factors, inner development for example, determine that). For me, up to a point, social status and a sense of worthiness or belonging (I'm a "successful entrepreneur"!) were definitely a factor. These days money is a way to follow my interests, for example by doing all the workshops and retreats that I do, and a way of expressing my beliefs, by investing in startups and projects I believe in.

Considering that people have a very wide variety of different needs, conscious and unconscious, around money, there is no possible system which is perceived as fair by everyone. I think this was an important realisation for us and is likely to be one for any company that implements open salary. I personally feel that this remuneration model, because of its nature, is likely to be overall fairer than hidden payroll, which one (or very few) people have an oversight of and decision power over. Generally, the biggest inequalities need to stay hidden to survive as most people would be outraged to see them for what they are.

This is why, in my view, the gender and socioeconomic pay gap can be eliminated in companies which choose open salaries. If the responsibility is distributed and the complexity widely acknowledged, there is more of a chance to implement something which is fairer than the alternatives. Importantly, open pay is a consequence of the belief that people are fundamentally good and wired to care about one another. If that's not what you believe as a founder or a person of influence in your company, you will struggle with what I'm proposing. The pay system is a consequence of culture, which is a consequence of lived beliefs.

# Our Journey Towards Self-Set Pay

These days we are at a point where our culture – and therefore the pay system that is a small part of it – more or less upholds itself. But we haven't always been there. There was a time we had no idea who we were and what we stood for. Like many companies out there, we collated a list of what we thought were our values, printed them on a fancy poster and congratulated ourselves on a job well done. This had little to do with what was the everyday, lived reality of the company though.

I remember the day Dan and I got carried away about what the little and culturally-inexperienced team we had could pull through, and decided to implement the self-set pay we only just read about in *Maverick!* by Ricardo Semler. If he could do it in the 1980s with a team of thousands in a heavily-unionised manufacturing industry in Brazil, then surely we could do it in a small company which was part of the bleeding edge (or so we thought) startup culture of the 21st century in London. Things went pear-shaped very quickly. Our first full-time employee wanted to raise his salary significantly, without considering the bigger picture, and I panicked. We realised we expected our people, like many founders do, to know what to do in a process they've never been through.

The experience with self-set pay helped us to reset our expectations – and quickly. We invited people from different parts of the team (we had perhaps ten or twelve staff at the time), and with different levels of experience in the company, to form part of the pay committee that decided on salaries across the board. Daniel and I purposely stayed out of it as we didn't want to meddle in the process that commenced. During the next couple of months, The Moneypennys, as they were branded, did a vast piece of work we were ignorant about when we first decided to implement self-set pay.

Firstly, they researched what was reasonable for a company of our size, with limited resources (we've never raised investment and relied solely on client revenues) to spend on salaries altogether. Pretty essential stuff. Before, we had had a third/third/third model which dictated a third of our profits would be allocated to employee bonuses, a third would be reinvested in company growth, and a third would be paid to shareholders (in practice, most of this pot ended up staying in the company so that additional resources could be deployed there). But this was so early in the life of the company, and with sky high profit margins (since the costs were extremely low), we hadn't done a wider research to compare this with models other companies had and the amounts they were spending on salaries.

Over the next two years a variety of new approaches were tried. The second iteration of the pay committee created a pay matrix, having considered two different models – American, which values performance above all, and Japanese, which favours seniority. It became clear there was a lot of room to play in, and a variety of factors to consider in terms of what mattered to us as a company. The overall metric we decided to favour was "impact and scope", i.e. looking at how much impact a given individual has on the company and at what breadth that impact is occurring.

As this proved hard to evaluate, the committee decided to favour complexity of one's job and the level of uncertainty they were facing every day while performing it. Typically more senior roles have higher levels of uncertainty where you are likely to face new scenarios with no blueprint more often and be forced to create new systems to deal with things. Aside from the above, the type and level of professional experience individuals have were considered as key factors determining the salary they were to receive.

Later on, a peer review system got implemented where every person in the company, Daniel and I included, were to be reviewed and placed on the pay scale, by three different people in the company, some working closely, and some not, with the reviewed person. And so, every team member wrote three reviews and received three. It was an important task for each reviewer to find out what complexity and uncertainty was involved in their colleague's role to place them on a scale correctly. (Professional experience both in the field and in the company itself were obviously easier to determine.) The pay committee received and collated all of the reviews, on top of other work. All in all, a huge chunk of a job ended up being performed by them at the time, and to a very high standard.

All of this prepared the groundwork for the cultural shift required for us to be able to, approximately two years later, adopt self-set pay, and holacracy as governance and operational system, and so give our people ultimate decision power over their future as a company.

In brief, holacracy (following Wikipedia) is defined as a method of decentralised management and organisational governance, where authority and decision-making are distributed throughout a set of self-organising teams rather than being vested in a management hierarchy. This doesn't mean hierarchy is absent in the context of holacracy. It exists within projects or teams (also known as circles) but remains fluid according to needs of the moment. Also, and importantly, hierarchy concerns work – or roles – as opposed to humans themselves. Hierarchy becomes decoupled from people. Because of this, holacracy encourages and, if implemented correctly, encodes agility, autonomy, a clear sense of responsibility and ownership of work into an organisation's teams.

It wasn't long before it dawned on Dan and me that we couldn't expect our team to go through a hugely complex process of setting their individual pay in a vacuum of relevant information, practices and guidance. This is why, when founders ask me for tips on implementing self-set pay, I usually advise them to ponder on whether their culture and current organisational consciousness can actually accommodate the transformation involved in this process. It's possible to do more harm than good, acting from the best intentions, if you're keen to press ahead without taking the bigger picture into careful consideration.

If you are starting a startup, first things must come first. Establish your brand, understand what you are trying to do, and why you want to do it. I still clearly remember the evening when GrantTree brand was created. Whilst emptying a cheap bottle of white wine in our home office Daniel and I threw ever more ridiculous ideas at each other. By the time I came up with "Rapid Lobster" and set out to convince him it sounded like a hip, strong brand, we could barely hold it together. "We Claim Ltd" also came up; it's just that when he first said it I understood "Weak Lame Ltd" and started squealing like a piglet, rolling on the floor of our kitchen. GrantTree might have been in fact the only "boring" proposition of the evening. When we sobered up, it became clear that's what we were going with. Back then, there was little vision beyond wanting to prove to ourselves the idea was actually worth pursuing. And so we did.

# The Punter's World

They say that in the corporate context, behind every fabulous businesswoman there's at least one very powerful businessman... who is trying to stop her. It's not like that in the show business though. Behind every fabulous showgirl, there is at least one man who worships and champions her, no matter what. He gives her reassurance when she doubts herself, balances her and keeps her safe. It's not a sugar daddy I'm talking about. It's her inner masculine part, the animus (as opposed to the feminine principle, the anima) as Jung called them. Of course, this man can also be manifested externally, as a supportive boyfriend, accepting father or even an exceptionally generous punter.

Dita Von Teese recalls that early on in her career, when she still performed in second-rate joints, regardless of the environment she really cared to maintain her classy, true diva-like stage image. Her costumes were more elaborate and acts better thought through compared to those of the other girls. Shockingly, she chose to not bare all for the finale which earned her some condemning whistles from the audience on one hand but most certainly made her stand out on the other. After her act, when a tipping jar was passed around, which is still the case in less classy joints today, most punters would refrain from a contribution ("She didn't show her tits!"). There would always be one man though who put $100 bill in the jar, more than making it up for all the others who chose to pass. Dita says it was worth performing the act for this man alone.

The business world has a long legacy of being out of balance, even more so, in my view, than other parts of the world we've created together over centuries. Many believe the very principles of doing business, starting and scaling companies, come from the masculine. There's definitely some truth in that. Without the penetrative, strong-willed quality that strives to impose something on reality as it is, that disrupts in order to make space for the new and isn't afraid to piss off quite a few people in the process, few entrepreneurs can succeed. I observe, and respect, this trait particularly in the technology world.

The startup scene sometimes feels to me like a mad dog race though. Apparently there's plenty of food when you reach the end of the race, there's anything you've ever wanted. It's a long way to run but surely, with enough stamina, plus other dogs around and guys with the money egging you on, it's worth it? A lot of people, more and more in fact, tend to think so. Once you're in the race, it can sometimes get a little confusing why you're doing this but the race keeps going. It's addictive and a hell of a ride, even when the going gets tough. You feel on track, though. You feel useful. You know it's the right way to be. This is what you wanted when you quit that job. So let's go.

Soon enough it becomes clear the food is further out than you thought. Most drop dead on the racetrack, sooner or later. It's littered with dead bodies but no one pays much attention to them because every time one bites the dust, three new shiny puppies appear round the corner, running ahead, hungry. Why waste time being concerned by those choking in the dust while there's so much life around to celebrate, making jolly noise as it passes by?

Some get to the food, having completed the race which seems to lead through a thick jungle, where even more drop dead trying to find the lost track. The thing is, once you're this far out, after all the running and, quite often, following the decisions made to find a shortcut of the track and to get ahead of the others, everything tastes off. Often you don't feel like enjoying the food that's now in front of you anymore. Instead, you grab it and scatter it around the jungle, maybe for others to pick up somewhere along their way. Perhaps it'll taste better to them? You spend time licking the inside of your paws, howling to the moon at night. Everything that seemed deeply meaningful at the beginning of the race is now distant and foggy. Some choose to run again, to a different part of the jungle (maybe the food's better there), some stop and find a cave to sleep in, sometimes never to come out.

This is just one perspective on the startup world, one of many I can give, and yet one that feels right to bring up now. Being part of the startup scene has sometimes, particularly at the beginning, felt like proving to the world that I don't care what it thinks. I set my own standards to prove things that really matter to me, in my own world. But this is just another leash with which to tie down my inner beast. What makes me curious is what might happen if the leash weren't there at all. Is the fear of the unknown all that's ever driven me to do anything? This is precisely why my inner masculine needs my inner feminine, the doing aspect of me needs the being aspect in order for my life to feel meaningful. This is also true in the collective space of the startup world – in many cases it has decoupled doing from being, gotten out of balance and is now facing the consequences.

# A War Of Distortions

My last full-length act (already mentioned above) created before I chose to retire from burlesque to pursue other creative hobbies – I still never say never to an occasional gig – was a truly delicious exploration of my inner conflicted polarity, a distorted masculine and a repressed, manlike feminine. I wanted to explore what it might be like to play both genders in one act and to create a conflict between them. The theme of the night was superheroes. At that time I was receiving a lot of spam emails (which you might recognise too!) from a company relentlessly marketing a penis enlargement medication branded MEGADICK. I knew at once this had to be my superhero's proud name. I purchased a superhero outfit, a little similar to Batman's, and later got it amended by a friend so as to come off easily and include MEGADICK spelled in fat letters across the chest. I also recorded the Megadick-female's (in clever disguise) voice and comments on video so that, using a projector, she could interact with Megadick-male, live on stage. The two engaged in a real time gangsta rap battle performed to *Gangsta's Paradise* to determine who is the "real thing" and who is merely a usurper. Towards the end the two also did a competitive strip dance where the female revealed large fake nipples (pasted on top of my real ones!) and a huge fake bush, while the male sported rich chest hair, created out of an afro wig, and a big cock made with a stuffed nude stocking, attached to a nude thong. Once the clothes were off, even though he laughed her off as a female (who can be female and a "real" superhero?!), eventually the victory was hers. Instead of resting on her laurels, mindful of the practicalities of her job, she decided to imminently set off to another part of the galaxy to sort out yet another crisis.

We live in a world of angry women. We live in a world of confused men. We live in a world where yin-yang polarity is all tangled up, but not because the feminine is becoming more like the masculine and vice versa. What seems to be happening instead is that the feminine as well as the masculine are losing their centre or their essence, which is where I tend to agree with the arguments of David Deida, an author and a motivational speaker, infamous for his work *The Way Of The Superior Man*. Deida's teachings, even though focused on personal, spiritual and sexual mastery, can also be applied to how we behave, lead and interrelate in the workplace. In this work I purposefully reference those from outside the relatively tight spectrum of famous – and often over-quoted – business authors. We cannot be true innovators if we rely only on widely known and accepted wisdom. Plus, isn't it more fun to learn, or to read, something new?

Coming back to the blurring of boundaries, as mentioned above, we are losing the natural polarity between the two aspects, manifested both internally and externally. Distorted feminine (using sky-high expectations and manipulation in order to magnetise that which she desires) and distorted masculine (action and penetration for their own sake, not as an act of service to higher values) show up instead. The masculine in its essence doesn't need to prove anything to himself or to the rest of the world. The feminine in its essence doesn't need to manipulate in order to magnetise.

Naturally, this dynamic shows up in a variety of ways in the world of business. Personally, I've spent most of my career in the space of the distorted masculine (as defined by Deida). Underneath my relentless drive and ambition I just wanted to feel a sense of belonging to the startup scene and have the recognition of my peers. Digging deeper, I wanted to feel that I have a right to be here. I matter because of what I do. I think many of us, women and men, spend our lives in this place, fighting for an inner right to exist, convinced that it's something that actually gets granted us one sunny day when we're deemed worthy (by whom or what, no one knows). For some, success comes, and with it some amount of social acknowledgement, but the sense of lack persists. Until, one day there's an inkling, and finally a knowing that a sense of belonging is not something that rests somewhere outside of us, and can be found or earned, like a treasure chest buried underneath a mountain of effort, tests and trials. No one but myself can give me this, by noticing it was already true. Seeking it outside is futile and always was. The knowing often comes wrapped up in anger, or a sense of betrayal. Why did no one tell me?!

Unfortunately, it is not something that can be told. I sense this particular kind of treasure-hunting energy around some of my ambitious friends and colleagues and I know I can do nothing to make their path easier, just like no one could have persuaded me of this earlier. I still notice craving for social acknowledgement from time to time. This is how I know I haven't fully embraced my inherent right to *be* in this world. The fact that I am here means that I am already wanted. There is nothing to earn. This is a key transition my inner masculine must go through in order to hone in on his real power. It feels a little like a rite of passage, a boy learning what it actually means to be a man.

When it comes to my inner feminine, I've also spent some of my life in the space of distortion, trying to find outside that which I lacked on the inside. I've built up expectations on what a "real man" is supposed to be and feel like, on what my wedding night was going to be like, on how I would be held and cherished by men in my life forevermore. And I was in for a surprise. Firstly, there are no "real men", the way we – women, who operate from a distorted, wounded place – picture them. It's a fantasy designed to project inner pain on to a perceived lack of good guys ("there are no good guys anywhere anymore" – how many times have I heard this!) in the outer world.

Lastly, am I held and cherished by men in my life like I've always wanted to be? Yes and no. I receive a lot of gifts of love and attention. And also, the men in my life are intelligent and mature enough to know it's not their job to hold me, or even to make me feel desirable. If anything, their eyes and actions are a mirror for how much I'm able to cherish myself. And more, how much compassion I can have for all the pieces of me that make me cringe when I see them.

# The Internal War

Roughly half of GrantTree believes we're not doing enough to be truly commercially successful (we are sustainable and growing but could of course be doing better). The other half feels that given our values and aspirations we aren't quite going all in to really embody them. The interesting thing is that not everyone is firmly on one side or on the other. Some, like me, agree with both. The split seam runs vertically through our bodies and our energy reserves. There's the feminine's longing for wholeness, the masculine's concern for the practical (sustainability and impact on the world) and the distorted masculine's fear that we'll be left behind when we're trying to accomplish all these things – by the competition, by our market, by the whole world.

I see this a lot on the startup scene, the dream to be different, the fear kicking in as the company grows and practical realities kick in. The expansion and unshakeable belief I – the founder – can create and sustain what I'm longing for in the world. Then, the contraction and the doubts about whether a successful company can really be scaled in a different way to the traditional model of the distorted masculine (essentially: bullying people into performance) as investors' agendas and market pressures start to apply.

As I look at the wider world, I see exactly the same dynamics playing out, on a much bigger scale, and so not as obvious. One group of people (or faction, or movement) calls us back to love, to connection with ourselves and the planet. Another warns we're so far down the wrong route we must take action, NOW, regardless of what feelings are at play, and each take our responsibilities towards the environment and one another very seriously. And, of course, the third one which prefers to mock one or both of the other two, mock everything that moves or breathes, in order to forget the bomb of fear it sits on. And so we dance, pulled in different directions within and without.

# Stage Blood vs. Real Blood

Every self-respecting stripper will have a good Halloween act ready to go and be booked by promoters around that time of the year. If you go for a morbid bride classic you're likely to spend days searching through charity shops for a neat vintage (of course!) wedding gown you'll then deliciously ruin with some fake blood and a couple of rips perhaps (to make it look like you literally just climbed out of your grave, naturally). Underneath it though you might have something really cacky (which stands for smutty or lascivious in a burlesquer's dictionary) or even, perhaps, a tiny G-string and nipple pasties covered in even more fake blood. If being a bride is not quite your thing, you might opt for embodying a sex-crazed witch, a vampire, or a horny ghost, anything Halloweeny enough really. Whatever it ends up being, stage blood is likely the first item on your shopping list.

In the world of businesses, it's not fake blood which makes the news. Roughly once a week somewhere in London town there's a tube disruption due to a body on the tracks. Having lived here since 2006 I seem to notice a trend that the folks who announce the disruption cause on a loudspeaker have become gradually less and less bothered to beat about the bush. Maybe it's simply a matter of coincidence and what announcements I've heard though. I think that I like it. I like hearing the truth that a delay is due to "a person under a train, apologies for any inconvenience to your travel today". I'm not glad that there is a body on the tracks, to be clear, I think that it's tragic. But I like hearing the truth, for this is where we are as a population. And there's no point in hiding from it. After all, it's already true, regardless of what we do with it.

I conjecture the majority of tube jumpers suffer from what the social system likes to neatly brand as "work-related stress". In this context, I would personally prefer the term perversion.

Work-related perversion that robs people of their dignity and often doesn't honour their rights as humans. Are employers to blame? Looking at this from a perspective of being one myself, I recognise a big chunk of responsibility but I also don't think it's all on us. As a society we've created a system which employers, employees and larger bodies like governments all choose to uphold – more often than not, merely by complying to what's considered standard.

It's a system where it's considered right and proper for people not to be trusted with things like access to company information, including financial information and salaries paid to fellow workers. This information is used instead as a tool in political battles. It's also a system where people are either indirectly encouraged, or do it through a choice of their own, to create a mask that hides all that's truly human – vulnerability, confusion, darkness, grief. A strong expression of any kind, even excitement or joy, is likely to not fit within the productive worker paradigm. Some people, having worked for decades with the mask on, *become it*, because the split is too difficult to endure. Everybody they interact with is then measured according to how useful they can be. "What do you do?" becomes a matter of how useful can you be to me, in this moment or in the future, as part of my meticulously-constructed masterplan to achieve my work or life-related goals. If you're not useful, I don't notice you.

In a better case scenario, work is a relatively harmless environment one chooses to participate in, in order to achieve a little freedom in other areas of life. We sacrifice three-quarters of our lifetime so that we can have enough money to pursue a hobby or to raise a family, maybe go on holiday now and then. And we make ourselves believe this is all there is to life – if we did not, our hearts would break. A lot of us contemplate on our deathbeds why we didn't give ourselves permission to live authentically (as per *Top Five Regrets of the Dying* by Bronnie Ware).

When I walk the streets of London, particularly the City (my own office is based just outside of it), I sense the presence of a huge beast in the collective space. It's not an elephant in the room, it's a dinosaur in the workplace. We've outgrown, a long time ago, the working structures within which most of us still operate. They don't respond to our levels of consciousness as individuals and the changing – some very urgent – needs of the world we inhabit. Yet we cling to what we know because change feels risky and scary.

## My Inner Man Says

I'm depressed. Particularly when I read the reports. They are mostly men. Three times as many men as women commit suicides in general and 64% of tube jumpers are male and disproportionately young. It's the guys who feel they need to keep up the game at all costs. Giving up equals a deeply personal failure on a most fundamental level. If I can't endure this like the others, there must be something deeply wrong with me. So wrong, that I'm perhaps simply unfit for this life and what it demands.

There must be a different way.

## My Inner Woman Says

I feel the City in my body sometimes when I meditate. I feel the despair and the anguish of all those locked in jobs that drive them insane, but they don't believe there's a different way. The mortgage needs to get paid and the expensive lifestyle sustained at all costs, so they spin in the hamster wheel of insanity. Until, one day, they cannot take it any longer and the easiest way out is to jump on the tracks. When I focus in meditation, I can feel all the lives that are hanging by a thread. The decisions to check out permanently which are about to be taken. And I grieve for all despair and madness, for the dis-ease of the City.

There must be a way out, a softening that brings a change

we're crying out for.

## My Inner Voice of Fear Says

This is life, people. And life is the survival of the fittest – it's always been this way, as per the evolution theory. And so it's ridiculous to presume that something should change and that it will change. Those who push on past their limits, when others are not prepared to, survive in tough conditions – it's the fundamental law of the universe. This one thing is clear to me, among all the other things that aren't. And so, my mission will always be to outsmart the others in an environment where only some of us can survive.

I am the one who is awake. I am the one who is vigilant. I am the one who is faithful. I am the only friend you can rely on. I am the only true lover you'll ever have. So, face the truth and let me get on with the job of keeping you alive.

## My Inner Adult Says

There is a different way indeed. It comes with being deeply grounded and secure ourselves to start with. Yes, lives have been lost and are being lost every week. Begin by cherishing yours.

The softening, Inner Woman, comes from welcoming the fear, anxiety and even despair as companions on the journey, a normal part of the multifaceted experience we call life. Now is the time, Inner Man, to give up playing the game. In the bigger scheme of things, it doesn't matter and it never has. Also, it's time to discover there has never been anything wrong with you. You are worthy and you are whole, as long as you're not on a mission to outsmart others, Inner Fear, but want to look after your community and protect them, other than just protecting yourself. We rise together, when those most vulnerable (yes, those whose lives are hanging by a thread) are noticed and gently taken by the hand.

# When the Hustle Takes Over (Or: On Startups And Personal Identity)

When you're on and off stage as a showgirl, the difference can be drastic to a point people actually don't recognise you! If that's the case, you're likely to have done your job right. It's all about the big reveal of who you are when you truly shine your unapologetic, in-your-face, glamorous, fantabulous light, and you only give enough to be begged for more by the punters. As soon as the reveal is done, a satin robe is on and if they want more, well, they are likely to need to pay more! In some circles it's even considered a bad omen to prance around in your (more covered) costume before or after the show. Your identities as the stage goddess and a party girl are very much different and should not meet too often. Which isn't the case with startup founders.

A founder friend of mine recently shared how easy it is to merge completely with your business, particularly at the beginning of the journey, when you feel guilty for doing anything that isn't directly, and ideally immediately, adding value to the startup. It's easy to start feeling guilty doing almost anything that doesn't in some way add value to your company. Having cast my mind back to the beginnings of GrantTree, I clearly remember the days when the entirety of me and my world would literally hang on the success of the venture. I was nothing else but what I accomplished. My sense of self, worthiness and belonging on this planet and in this body rested on the business that I chose to start at 25. How frightening.

Since I've started to operate in the startup world, I've seen plenty of people succeed and fail. Naturally, more of the latter just because it's about nine times statistically more likely (depending on what data you look at). Whatever happens, their identity often gets destroyed having been sucked into their startup. Let me explain. In the first (and more likely) scenario, I am what I do and the venture fails. I might as well die. Everything I ever wanted to do to create a dent in the world, express myself, improve the reality I live in, and leave me financially affluent to pursue fun things that cost money, is gone. I have no right to be here. Many first-time entrepreneurs who fail feel that way. Some take the belief they have no right to be here to extreme conclusions. I grieve deeply reading about suicides amongst unsuccessful entrepreneurs.

The fact entrepreneurs tend to suffer from mental health and well-being problems is recognised by research such as this performed in 2015 by a clinical professor and entrepreneur by the name of Dr Michael Freeman. Out of 242 entrepreneurs surveyed a whopping 49% reported having a mental condition with depression being present in 30% of cases, followed by ADHD (29%) and anxiety problems (27%). By comparison, only 7% of the general US population identify as depressed according to the National Center for Health Statistics.

Likewise in the UK in 2018, the NatWest Great British Entrepreneur Awards conducted its *Mental Health in Entrepreneurship* survey, with 100 entrepreneurs taking part. It found that 58% of those surveyed experienced mental health issues with conditions including anxiety (21%), depression (19%) and stress (41%). Moreover, 55% of respondents said that running a business has had a negative impact on their mental health.

In the second (and less likely but still possible) scenario, the venture succeeds and I, hereby, am granted the right to carry on existing. My sense of identity as a "successful entrepreneur" is now reinforced, the straitjacket gets tighter. I end up worrying about how much of my ability to love myself is connected to the creation I am now identified with. Surely, without it, I'm absolutely nothing. I feel relatively good about myself (after all, I am a success!) but only to a point. Is this really the end of everything I dreamt of, everything I wanted to express, everything I could create? If so, maybe I'm vastly limited, and in consequence, unworthy, after all. I remember feeling completely destroyed as I poured savings, buckets upon buckets of energy, my innocence and childlike idealism into my business, to receive some feedback from a temporarily frustrated colleague that "things suck over here". Now I know it was never anybody else's job (in terms of delivering good feedback and acknowledgement) to give me a sense of being a worthy human. I am grateful this realisation came before I considered taking drastic actions many talented and idealistic businesspeople, feeling betrayed and deeply unappreciated by the world around them, do.

I know some people who jump from one venture to the next, determined to be successful at all costs. Success becomes a drug and it's necessary to get one fix after another, so as not to be alone with what's true when no signs of external acknowledgement are there to distract us. And that's a lot of dark stuff to process and a lot of fundamental questions to sit with (other than to answer, because when I'm ready to be present with the dark depths of my being, answers are never obvious). Some serial entrepreneurs get stuck on the treadmill of success, subconsciously, because there's too much at stake to stop. And when they eventually do, because poor health catches up with them for example, there is too much darkness and fear or anxiety to process, and everything turns black.

I grieve deeply reading about depression and suicides amongst successful entrepreneurs. Those who sold their businesses to discover they are nothing without them, or those who could never leave them for the fear that's what they would discover.

Two years ago, I reduced my workload at my ten-year-old company to three days a week. This action was surrounded by a lot of shame as I felt a misguided sense of responsibility and obligation towards my awesome team (who am I, some posh c*nt, to work less than them!). It was made easier by the fact that my mental well-being and energy levels deteriorated significantly, probably to create space for transformation that ensued and is still in progress. If it weren't for the fact that I was physically and mentally too weak to be in the office every day, I don't think I would have ever given myself permission to step back. (Generally, over the years in business, the weaker and less capable I felt, the more shameful and guilty about it I became, and therefore the more inclined to push myself to work even harder to hide the fact I felt weak to begin with.) Most importantly, if the company hadn't been ready in terms of appropriate structures and systems in place, and many talented people working in it, my working less wouldn't have been possible at all.

Today, I feel grateful to myself, to my business partner, our new CEO, Nicky, and to the rest of my colleagues that the decision to work part time was well received. If it hadn't been, I would have found a way (being in an unstable place that I was in) to blame myself for the "weakness" of wanting and needing to work less. Internally, I was shivering with shame. To a point that when a kind female colleague expressed excitement about what I might do with the two weekdays that are now unaccounted for, it felt too overwhelming to admit I was going to sleep, meditate and seriously look after the needs of my inner child, with a level of commitment I'd never done before in my life. This felt, and continues to feel, like a hugely important piece of work.

Today, I am free. I've given myself permission to feel and not to do anything at all, if staying with the truth of my inner experience consumes all the energy available, and sometimes it does. I am free to discover who I am when there's no agenda, what moves within me, whether it's dark or light. Which doesn't mean that responsibilities and commitments I have taken on are suddenly not important to uphold. I am grateful for having those and for the fact they keep me grounded. I recognise, however, that I am vastly more than the "startup identity" I had created for myself to help me hide from aspects of my being I'd rather not engage with – even if that's where I ultimately need to go in order to access my greatest power; and bring this power back into my business. I realise that I'm blessed with the degree of freedom I have and sincerely wish all of you who engage in starting and scaling companies to be able to create such freedom for yourselves. I'm grateful to my intelligent and resourceful team but also acknowledge my own impact, resilience and stamina which allowed me to help develop the company to its current shape over the last ten years.

"Out of office" burlesque act as performed at Madame Jojo's

# Part Two

# The Feminine Rising And Leadership Of The Future

# Can Marriage Be Sexy?

Marriage is a word which, next to "stripper", also carries a dense energetic imprint. For many, it's outdated as a paradigm of relating, it belongs to the past. For others, it carries frustration, disappointment, even shame and a sense of pure evil (forced marriage, child marriage). No wonder we shy away from using it. As GB Shaw put it at the beginning of the last century

> *[W]hen two people are under the influence of the most violent, most insane, most delusive, and most transient of passions, they are required to swear that they will remain in that excited, abnormal, and exhausting condition until death do them part.*
> – GB Shaw, preface to *Getting Married*, 1908

That is what marriage 110 years later amounts to for a lot of people of my generation who live in Western Europe. According to statistics quoted by Business Insider in May 2019, the marriage rate decreased from 72% of US adults in 1960, to 50% in 2017. So much for marriage between two people. Similar dynamics apply, on a much subtler level, when it comes to the inner marriage – or integration – of the feminine and masculine principle in a wholesome individual. It's only once the two principles come together within us that they can unite in the outer world of our work, in organisations and communities of all sorts – and particularly those where the commercial agenda is of some importance.

Having been in a partnership for ten years (and in a marriage for more than half of that time) I believe that a commitment to growth, and a commitment to truth, is what's required for any long-term relationship to stay alive. This by no means guarantees that it will last of course. The truth for many radically self-honest people in my circle meant that at some point a relationship they cherished had to end. I cannot know exactly how my own truth will challenge me with regards to relating with others in the future. What I do know is that it's likely to keep challenging me. And I'm committed to continue giving it my very best shot.

Globally speaking, right now we're standing before a challenge possibly unlike any other in human history. The feminine and the masculine paradigms in organisations of all kinds – from families, through local communities to small businesses and multinational corporations – must come together if our world is to survive. As writer Jocelyn Mercado points out, there is an ancient South American prophecy about the Eagle and the Condor. Long ago, human societies decided to become two different types of people: the Eagle people who are typically mind-oriented and industrial, and the Condor people who are intuitive, creative, and prioritise the heart above the brain, and mysticism over rationalism. Both are needed in order for humans to be successful as a species. For centuries, however, the world has been out of balance with the civilisation dominated by qualities representing an extreme, unhealthy version of the Eagle people. If the two aspects of the human consciousness – the Eagle and the Condor – don't come together in peace and unity, our civilisation will perish.

Another writer, Arkan Lushwala, known for his books *The Time of the Black Jaguar* and *Deer and Thunder*, argues – based on indigenous teachings and his experience of working with indigenous tribes – that when we return to a balance between the wholesome masculine and feminine within, we can become tree-like, deeply rooted, connected to the Earth. Lushwala, heralded "a rare indigenous bridge of the global north and south", explains that it's only when we find the balance of these two forces within that we lose our fear of expressing our truest selves, each individual bringing their unique contribution into the world.

The fact we are way out of balance couldn't be more obvious

when it comes to issues such as climate change. Needless to say, this is also the case in the modern world of work, where masculine energy, often in its distorted form, has been dominant possibly ever since the Industrial Revolution. This is also the reason why in these pages, I prefer to call on the wisdom of people such as Lushwala, an Andean ceremonial leader, as opposed to conventional business leaders and authors. A new, expanded perspective is needed in a world where productivity and output have superseded intuition, receptivity and creativity. We are on the brink of a vast and important change but there's no blueprint for how this is to happen. We can though, and we must, trust our inner guidance, stemming from the integration of feminine and masculine principles within ourselves as individuals to begin with. For me personally it's been – and continues to be – one of the most amazing adventures of all growth-related challenges I've faced, as this book hopefully demonstrates.

Let's explore the feminine aspect in a bit more depth. Whether we are talking about the inner feminine (present in us regardless of gender) or the outer feminine leadership force manifested out in the world, it tends to attract and invite the masculine polarity. The masculine part holds space for the feminine part and creates safety. However, it comes easily to the masculine aspect to get into a distortion, which is when he becomes ego-driven, controlling and dominating over the feminine instead of working in harmony with her. It's easy for the distorted version of the feminine – on the other hand – to manipulate the masculine so that he does exactly what she wants, instead of trusting his higher purpose. A thousand things between them can go wrong and do, inside of ourselves, in one-to-one relationships, in larger communities, and in commercial organisations. Balance – or union, the "tantric marriage" – of both aspects requires radical honesty and continuous vigilance. The equilibrium requires time to build and takes little to become distorted.

What do organisations with a good balance of masculine

and feminine look like? And what does it really take for a deep, ecstatic union between them to be able to emerge? There isn't much evidence but I personally know a few fellow entrepreneurs who are consciously on this journey, even if the above aren't necessarily the terms and phrases they would use to describe it. For example, in one coaching company I know decisions are collectively "felt into", taking into consideration embodied sensations, rather than intellectually thought through. In another, important decisions on the governance level are only made once there's harmony, positivity and love flowing between individuals responsible for making them. If that's not happening, getting back to a state of harmony in the collective field becomes the priority. In these companies, and many others I've come across, the essence and consciousness are intertwined. The values and higher purpose are married to the commercial agenda. The action goes hand in hand with awareness or reflection. At GrantTree we often use a check-in protocol at the beginning of meetings which means we go around the table and everyone (if they want to) gets to say how they feel or, in other words, what they bring into the meeting. It could be frustration – or any other feeling – to do with the topic at hand or something completely unrelated, such as emotions to do with a personal life event. This process helps us acknowledge our humanity and to be present with the entirety of life. Plus, very often, to be more efficient with what needs to get done as emotions running in the background have been brought on to the surface and acknowledged.

The following sections talk more about the feminine and masculine leadership centres and how to integrate them, in order to help you find balance between the polarities within your own leadership, both in personal and in professional life.

# Find Your Sass (Or: Leading From The Feminine)

No one more perfectly embodies the sass and the glamorous shining confidence of the feminine than a stripper, regardless of their gender (and I've seen quite a few fabulous male and non-binary strippers in my time!). It's all about stage presence and responsiveness to the audience's feedback in real time. Most strippers (at least those in the world of burlesque) have an act prepared and know what and how they are going to present on stage. Still, there's also the great unknown of what the energy will be between them and the audience when the time comes. Maybe some jokes will be missed while others are unexpectedly welcomed with a roar of laughter. Therefore, a good stripper learns quickly to tune in to their surroundings and be super responsive so the magic of a well-received act can happen.

It's obvious to me that collectively we are trying to integrate a different paradigm of leadership. We're stomping in the dark and so it feels confusing. That's where strippers can be our best teachers! We need to learn to be more in tune with what our careers and businesses *feel like* as opposed to what logically makes sense according to a paradigm designed by someone else or what our parents would have wanted for us. We may then discover that, as long as our essential needs are met, the level of material wealth has little to do with whether we can gain a deeper sense of belonging in the world, or an abundance and joy felt within. Because of this it starts to make sense to go with the inner feeling of what's right for us, with what feels good and flowing in our bodies. It's a completely different and new kind of knowledge and attunement, often at odds with the rational inquiry we're used to. Truth be told, I still sometimes struggle with switching from one to the other or, what feels like the ultimate art – seamlessly integrating one with the other.

According to healer and founder of the School of Intuitive Studies Wendy De Rosa, feminine energy is rising, and with it our intuition and trust of the inner call to speak the truth. But what does it mean to lead from the feminine, in the context of our inner leadership (or self-leadership)? For me, attunement to what's actually going on (as opposed to what I think should be going on), and compassion for whatever I find, are always a good start. It's a bottom-up perspective, meaning that I listen first to what's present in my system, where the energy seems to want to flow. I don't impose any goals or agendas on myself (which would be very tempting to do from a masculine perspective). My only intention is to stay present with what's currently alive within me. This in itself can be a hell of a task since the things which are actually "alive" and wanting to be seen, underneath the layers of "keeping it together", can be challenging.

As an example, I had a significant "down time" as part of my personal journey in the last year and it's precisely then that I had to hone in on my feminine leadership. I felt a lot of fear and confusion as I let go of different structures and identities I'd created to feel safer in the world, and intellect didn't seem like a particularly helpful tool to see me through this. In fact, allowing even fairly neutral thoughts in often felt painful, as there was already plenty for my system to process. It felt like structures and patterns I could rely on in the past weren't accessible (or felt useless) and so I needed to create a new opening, or a new way of relating to what was going on.

And so I learnt to trust, with hiccups at first, my energy and my body. I slowly changed perspective from "I need to hold, shape, and push my life along to make the most of it" to "my life is holding, shaping and leading me, possibly to make the most of who I can become". For some of you this perspective will seem difficult to accept and I hear you. It seems to me to be very important in the context of leadership from the feminine, though. How can I allow the bigger picture to simply unfold, including influences way beyond my control? How can I trust it has the power to "solve" me – rewire the way I relate to myself and the wider world, instead of relying on myself to solve anything? Some say, "Be careful what you choose to write about." I'm pretty sure it applies to anything else connected to a conscious effort in life. At some point while writing this book a part of me knew I was going to go through an initiation into the essence of feminine leadership, so I would have a much better grasp of what I'm talking about. When it came, it was significant and anything but glamorous. Everything seemingly fell apart, my confidence in what I had to say dwindled, my motivation to keep up with the progress I'd already achieved with the writing disappeared. I wasn't even sure what the core of my message was anymore. Somehow, by staying present with the chaos within me, I was gradually, slowly, shown the next steps.

It was in a similar way that I got the inspiration to start writing this book in the first place. It came from conversations, messages I received from others, a sense of curiosity or inner calling, without expectation. I became aware of a few publishing contacts through friends and my network, and things started unfolding. It feels important to say that at some point I surrendered the outcome of whether this book was to see the light of day to a force bigger than me. I knew life would decide if it was worthwhile and an important enough contribution to business thinking to be published or read. I wasn't attached to the outcome of being a published author anymore, even though that was still what a part of me desired. Who am I to know if perhaps there are different, better ways for me to contribute to the world?

Throughout that dark time, I maintained receptivity. I was present to what I felt, but also to how life moved around me. I learnt to receive attention and help from others without shame. I learnt I can be loveable when not productive or "fun". I understood what it means to listen deeper and choose

79

which things to do when resources are very limited. I found in myself deeper love and appreciation for friends around me, for coworkers, for circumstances in my life that supported me going through this process and made it possible. I committed to not take those people and those things, and my own capability to hold myself in productivity, and in sanity, for granted. To stop trying to figure things out rationally even though so much in me is yearning for an answer or an explanation. I learnt to lean towards that which wants to unfold naturally, and also to find some spaciousness within an inner contraction.

During the dark time, it also became apparent in how many ways I berate myself and am my own worst critic when in a vulnerable place. I judge myself horrendously for not being better at handling a crisis even though, objectively speaking, I'm actually doing a pretty good job. Creating space for this old patterning to change is, naturally, work in progress but the "down time" felt like a significant starting point. It may actually be some of the most important work I've done to date. This all makes me wonder whether it may be appropriate to rebrand "down time" to "power time" and encourage change for how we tend to think about times of reduced productivity and output in our lives. From the perspective of feminine leadership, it makes a lot of sense.

Just as our masculine goes on a journey that requires stamina and courage, so does the feminine, in her own unique way. Author Sharon Blackie contests Joseph Campbell's point that the feminine is the destination of the masculine. She has a journey of her own which involves trials of a different kind – and a descent into the dark. Her road of trials is a road into the centre of her being, into a sense of connectedness with everything that exists. While the hero must slay a dragon, the heroine would rather "engage with the dragon than kill him, entice him into her purposely diverse team, harness his unique skills." For her a dragon, just like other creatures of the dark, is a companion and an ally.

What's the heroine's destination then? As Blackie argues in *If Women Rose Rooted,*

> *In the Otherworld, the long, hard process of transformation has been initiated; fragmented and dismembered by her experience in the dark, she starts now by searching for the lost pieces of herself. She needs to reveal her strengths as well as to uncover her weaknesses, and one of the key purposes of her Journey is to break through what she perceives to be her own limitations, so that she can not only identify her unique gifts, but develop the resources necessary to use them. The Journey requires her to explore the source of her own belonging, find her centre, begin to recover an understanding of her own place in the great, connected web of the world. She is walking her way back into being. As in any pilgrimage, the path winds its way across unfamiliar, uneven territory, and this long, arduous Journey requires endurance, stamina and focus.*

The author likens this path to that of the centre of the spiral or a labyrinth. The heroine goes into the centre, or depths of her being, many times over to uncover new gifts and insights, and then goes outwards into the world bringing them with her. Her way is that of cycles leading her within and then without. This mysterious, non-linear journeying must become the familiar domain of anyone dedicated to the development of his or her inner feminine.

# Growing Bigger Ovaries (Or: Leading From The Feminine In The Business Context)

It's merely a stereotype that strippers and those who lead from the feminine energy cannot be effective in business. Because showgirls and table dancers are so good at tuning in to their audiences and delivering exactly what titillates them the most, they can get very successful quite quickly. Just check the history of burlesque and the fame and fortune of such stars as Josephine Baker, Bettie Page, Tempest Storm or Mae West. They were the absolute darlings of their time and are still a massive source of inspiration for modern strippers. They were, and remain, the queens of harnessing one's feminine power of seduction and ability to profit from their stage charisma.

As I mentioned in Part One, in one of my more recent, and more elaborate burlesque acts, a female superhero fights a male one, both embodied by me and also representing the two sides of me. I use a pre-recorded video projection allowing one superhero to interact with the other in real time in a gangsta rap battle (performed to the tune of *Gangsta's Paradise*). The male in this act is quite boisterous, laughing at the fact a female superhero would even exist, while the female simply wants to get the conflict over and done with to get on with her day-in-day-out business of saving the world. In the end, that's exactly what she gets to do.

I'm convinced that you cannot show up effectively in your feminine leadership in the context of running a company unless you've explored the feminine aspect in the space of your inner leadership. If you're not quite sure where to start, just stay with this inquiry and allow for it to lead you where it wants to, in the time that it chooses. If your saboteur or inner critic protests at the thought of this, seek a place of trust and restfulness in yourself.

Once you have a good grounding in what leading from the feminine part feels like on the inside, it's much easier to bring it into a community or an organisation. In many situations it's all about the awareness of what's present, in me and externally. It's about holding space, with attention, ideally loving attention, for what's unfolding. About allowing for all that needs to be seen (heard or spoken) to be seen. About observing your inner energy movement to stay in tune with the arguments or voices you're feeling drawn to, or sometimes, with those who have remained voiceless.

Being "drawn to" doesn't have much to do with rational argument, it's a gut instinct (or heart instinct) about what's important. Don't be surprised if it takes you a while to develop this skill, it's not something we're taught how to do. In situations with a lot of uncertainty and fear involved, it still takes me a while to bypass a part of me that wants to act fast, out of panic, in order to feel more in control, and to tune into these often subtle sensations deeper within.

I wouldn't really say leading from the feminine is about not acting. It's more about taking time to understand where the impulses to act come from in you. And also, it's about taking time to feel into different aspects of the situation at hand. Mystic, philosophy and theology scholar and creator of a worldwide spiritual movement Osho (also known as Bhagwan Shree Rajneesh) mentions in one of his lectures that the role of the feminine part is to absorb. It takes things in and transmutes them.

Are all difficult situations in business appropriate to act on from the perspective of leadership from the feminine part? Quite possibly not. Sometimes speed and decisiveness matter a lot. I can certainly recall quite a few instances where I *thought* this was the case at the time. Speed was needed more than anything else. From today's perspective, I know this was a fear-based perception. My inkling at this stage is that there's a place for feminine leadership in every situation of conflict or crisis, and particularly where there's stress, anxiety, potential judgement and fear involved. If you observe yourself thinking that there's absolutely no time to feel into things before acting, that is probably a great signal that now is the time to pause and take in the situation more fully.

According to one of the spiritual authors I follow, Alana Fairchild, feminine authority comes into place when power is tempered with mercy, wisdom, compassion and love. Empowerment trumps control. Through living your truth and integrity, you lead by authentic example, claiming your own power from within in every moment, rather than using "power" that was granted to you from elsewhere. In this paradigm, there's no sense of unhealthy responsibility for another, which creates dependency and disempowerment. What comes with the claiming of inner power is recognition of your authority which has nothing to do with your position in the external hierarchy, levels of social recognition or material success. When you step into your authority in the feminine way, your talents shine through. There's no shame and no need for false modesty on one hand or PR coverage on the other, you simply live what you are, on a level of deeply personal and embodied power.

It's because of the lack of feminine leadership that so many of us, often underneath all the signs of power and external success, feel completely disempowered and unworthy. An authentic sense of power can never be granted from elsewhere, and that's one of the key lessons of the feminine part. It's found deep within, underneath the chatter of the mind. It's a place of deep alignment with ourselves and, if you experience it that way, a power way bigger than you which feels transpersonal and universal. To me, it's beyond where we can go with mindfulness. It's a place of inner wholeness, in other words divinity. But you may experience or frame it differently and that's just as valid as what I experience. When you act from that place, there is no doubt or hesitation. There is just a gentle, non-urgent knowing which flows through you without effort. A sense of pristine clarity.

Within the paradigm of feminine leadership, hierarchy doesn't make much sense because underneath all the titles we are simply naked humans, with fears and traumas, but also unique strengths and talents. According to Anna Betz, a coach and author who writes about and studies collaborative leadership in organisations, including self-management and teal, the collective intelligence provides a new, qualitatively different source of leadership for organisations. In the age of the feminine power rising, this makes a lot of sense to me. We all have different flavours of awareness, ability and mastery and they can often be channelled more effectively when we come together. Those of you who have experience working on boards or panels know that there is a different and a surprising level of wisdom and insight that can emerge when a few people with inner authority come together with no ego-driven agendas.

To say more on leadership from the feminine aspect within us, we have admittedly, as Wendy De Rosa points out, hidden and covered up feminine energy by associating it with weakness. But the feminine principle is rising within all of us. We are, collectively, shedding shame, speaking truth and communicating with integrity. The masculine element within us (and within the collective field) is also waking up to how the feminine has been suppressed and objectified. The feminine has re-emerged as a wounded consciousness but is refusing to stay wounded – the healing process happens through courageous exposing of the truth, as seen in the #MeToo movement. When the feminine rises, it unearths whatever has suppressed or held us back and so may involve a challenging process. Ultimately though, both on the individual and on the collective level, the feminine rising points to liberation, permission to be our authentic selves and to live in truth.

# A Feather's Touch (Or: Key Principles Of Feminine Leadership)

When you lead from the feminine principle, you rest in the place of inner authority, not lent to you by hierarchy but harnessed from the core of your being. In other words, earned with self-knowledge and courage to get to know the entirety of who you are, darkness included. The journey of mastering the qualities of leadership from the feminine part is not as much a journey of knowledge, as it is one of opening. Those who are masters in this art aren't closed off to any perspectives, contracted in fear or limited in their ability to contain polarities. There is an inner flow, openness and flexibility that easily translates to how they deal with the outer world. It's beautiful to witness. And perhaps mastering leadership from the feminine part is above all about creating space in situations of contraction, relentless opening of closing doors. Mary Beard, Professor of Classics at Newnham College, Cambridge, points out in her little book *Women & Power* that we need to start thinking about power in a way that's decoupled from prestige, or in ways that are coded as male. It's all about thinking collaboratively, treating power as an attribute or even a verb ("to power") as opposed to a noun.

Many political fractions around the world today advocate division and some form or adversity towards the other. A is safe, while B is suspicious. We're good together over here as long as the walls are tall enough for us to have nothing to do with the folks over there. It's possibly the most effective way of stepping into power, underpinned by fear in large groups of people, known since ancient Romans. I remember learning about the principle they used – *divide et impera* (divide and rule) – back in primary school. Such a simple concept, yet still perfectly effective today. Fear and anger are powerful emotions which can connect and unite us. Particularly if they aren't fully conscious in the collective, it's easily tempting to use them for a desired political effect, as demonstrated time and time again over the last decade.

Leadership from the feminine principle, however, has no interest in power derived from fear and anger of the collective. That kind of power cannot achieve anything meaningful. It can help fulfil a particular agenda but it won't contribute to the advancement of humanity. The starting point of the kind of leadership I'm referring to is, again, openness to the other, invitation aimed at the other to step into their own power and partake in the complex task that leadership itself is. One who leads from the feminine part knows very well that the best thing they can do is to open up ways for power to flow in the collective, rather than limiting it. From my perspective, there's an enormous relief that comes from the knowledge my team are also invested in the success of GrantTree, like Daniel and I are. The fact that I'm good at hustling and getting a company off the ground doesn't mean I have all the skills needed to scale it. My business would never be what it is today if we didn't choose to create opportunities to distribute power early on, didn't continue to practise this over the years, and didn't explicitly reject the temptations of leadership through division.

I'm truly fascinated by how the concept of power changes in the context of leadership from the feminine principle. The ultimate power comes from surrender to powerlessness. This, when truly embraced, has dramatic consequences. The feminine leader within you already knows that a sense of control over your company or your life is an illusion. Of course, our choices do matter. We can move towards things that attract us and evolve past personal limitations. We can achieve things we previously thought were impossible. We can choose A over B and every choice we take has tangible consequences. Yet while these things are true, in the bigger scheme of things, the sense of control they may give us is an illusion. There are bigger forces and dynamics at play. The more I try to force things to go along with my plan, the more they resist. The more I'm in touch with myself, the more I recognise I'm happiest when tuned into guidance on where and how my talents are best used, surrendering and listening in other than trying to pursue a plan I created for myself. As I act from this place of attunement, things flow with me instead of resisting.

When you are prepared to move out of the way, and truly recognise your powerlessness, paradoxically a sense of deeper power and agency emerges. This doesn't happen instantaneously. You need to be prepared to sit with the silence within, and listen. More often than not, you'll be tempted to fill the silence with some sort of a plan or new agenda because it's very uncomfortable for my mind not to know. But if you hold out, sooner or later there's a sense of clarity about the next steps, which emerges from a place beyond your personal agenda, beyond your desire to be recognised as decisive and effective. As your inner journey evolves, and trust in yourself increases, you will start to move from a place of surrender and listening in more and more, both in life and in business.

What also emerges, or at least has done on my own journey of exploring the feminine, is a sense of lightness and playfulness. The feminine doesn't particularly care about the rules of social and political correctness, she flies above what's considered appropriate also in the business context. Just over a year ago, I got invited to join a prestigious panel of experts in the space of engineering and technology whose aim is to influence Government's policy for the benefit of the sector and to create thought leadership around key issues in the space. The invitation came directly from the panel's chairman and I was honestly a little confused to receive it. I even tried to send a senior member of our grants team instead as I felt I didn't have enough experience or expertise to offer. It didn't work, I learnt that the invitation was strictly personal. As I arrived at my first meeting of the panel in one of the stunning boardrooms of the Institute of Engineering and Technology, it turned out I was quite possibly the youngest person around the table. Even though a little intimidated by the calibre of my colleagues' leadership in the sector, I realised it was down to my inner sense of worthiness to decide whether or not I could add value. Needless to say, I decided that I could, and started to participate in the discussion with eagerness. One thing that still bugged me though was how I ended up in this prestigious group.

After the formal part of the meeting, we all enjoyed a beautiful three-course dinner in an adjacent dining room. It was then that the mystery was finally solved. I sat next to the panel's secretary who mentioned the chairman saw me deliver a "really engaging talk" at one of the industry conferences and decided to invite me to join the panel. Nothing would be extraordinary about this if it weren't for the subject of the talk, which was a variation of a TEDx I'd delivered earlier, titled *The Businesswoman and the Stripper*. The talk I gave, which the chairman saw and remembered, involved drawing parallels between what I learnt as an open-culture company leader and the skills I gained performing on nightclub stages as a burlesque diva. It was the first time, in this risqué talk, that I decided to bring these two very different aspects of my life and personality together and show up, with no care for political correctness, in the full spectrum of my talent and uniqueness. I received plenty of great feedback on my talk and yet it was an amazing surprise to learn that it also earned me a seat on IET's policy panel. The talk later became a cornerstone for the book you are holding.

As mentioned above, the road to mastering feminine leadership starts with finding and developing your inner authority. And this, in turn, is only possible through connecting with the entirety of your being, including the shadow aspects. So let's take a moment to step into the chamber of shadows.

# Entrepreneurship And BDSM

A lot of stripping acts have a kinky streak to them. Even Dita Von Teese herself, although generally considered one of the most glamorous performers worldwide, likes playing a damsel in distress and her famous illustrated book includes burlesque-related stories and photographs on one side, and "fetish and the art of the Teese" on the other. A bit (or quite a bit) of unconventional naughtiness simply goes well with a lot of stripping acts. So even during your standard cabaret night, you are likely to see elements of bondage or flogging (in a double act), suggestions of sexual submissiveness or – on the contrary – dominance in a given performer's get-up and stage presence. Many a motivated girl started her career as a performer only to realise her true interests (and considerably bigger financial rewards) were in being a professional dominatrix.

The interesting thing about kink, at least engaged with in a conscious way, is that it gives you an opportunity to consider your darkness in a container where you get to set the rules. By the same token, I noticed quite a while ago that my business was the most perfect mirror for my shadows and weaknesses. Pretty much any problem we were facing in the business could easily be translated to something that hasn't been resolved within me or within my relationship with Daniel.

It seemed fascinating, and so when I was once given a free rein as a speaker at a business conference, I delivered a rather risqué talk on the parallels between entrepreneurship and BDSM. One of the points I explored is that both of the above are fundamentally, albeit at a deep, not easily acknowledged level, about the exploration of shadows. Alongside some stunning Shibari photography (Shibari is the art of Japanese bondage), I decided to list my weaknesses and the business' problem areas on two different slides and compare them. This is what came up.

Personal darkness, past and present:

- depression (which I now understand as numbing darkness),
- resistance to routine,
- deep fear of chaos and confusion,
- controlling under pressure,
- sense of unworthiness/striving to be special,
- fear of breaking down mentally.

My business' darkness, past and present:

- lack of organisational awareness,
- lack of clarity on accountabilities and decision making,
- resistance to chaos as "unproductive",
- lack of Big Picture audacity/ambition,
- fear of breaking down commercially.

I'd like to think that as a business we've progressed in working on some of the areas mentioned above. This happened as a result of the conscious effort of quite a few people who saw their personal journey as aligned with the company's success, as opposed to simply my personal transformation.

Arguably, the company has its own life now, independent of mine or Daniel's. Also, as it grows into a mature organisation, its responsibilities – and its problems – are more complex and multifaceted than any we may be challenged with in our individual lives. Still, parallels between the personal and organisational shadow are impossible to miss. And I know the imprint of my shadows is strong. Perhaps strong enough to remain even as both people in the company and structures that govern it evolve way past my state of consciousness when the business started.

On the following slides, the razzmatazz show-woman in

me stepped in to re-quote CG Jung. He said and wrote plenty of things I resonate with. One of them, particularly in the age where so many people believe in "raising their vibration" other than descending into personal darkness, is this:

> One does not become enlightened by imagining figures of Light, but by making the darkness conscious (…) Shadow work is the path of the heart warrior.
> – CG Jung

Taking it into a business context, I chose to rephrase this thought in the following way:

> Your personal shadows are reflected back at you in your business, at scale, and result in a more spectacular damage than just in your personal life. Shadow work is the path of a conscious entrepreneur.

As I explore the chamber of shadows, more layers of shame become apparent. As I'm getting more skilled at being in my body and receiving guidance from it, I experience more resistance towards operating purely on the level of the intellect. And somewhere in me there's a belief – based on a behavioural pattern – that being in my business equals being in my head. I remember countless times I followed intellectual reasoning while the body was screaming, "No!" because performing and "keeping it together" were more important than anything else. Now I face a choice – and also a challenge – to find a way of being in the rational that's supported and powered by the embodied.

One of the ways I approach this is to seek guidance on business decisions I'm about to make with my "inner community". It's a beautiful, integrative way to acknowledge the power and wisdom of my body while inviting it to actively participate in the life choices I make. In this process, one is called to ask four different centres of one's body for guidance – the heart, the belly or the gut, the sex, and the head. I let them take turns and pay attention to what they have to say on a given issue, such as taking out a business loan for example. I imagine them as different characters sitting around a boardroom table, debating. If the decision is a complex and meaningful one, they are likely to disagree. For example, if I was considering taking out a cashflow loan with a personal guarantee, the head might reason it's not just desired but necessary, in order for expenses, and salaries in particular, to be covered. But there are other, likely more subtle voices present within me that also need to be heard. The heart, striving for connection, might hesitate: how will this impact people close to me? Am I taking into account the additional strain on my marriage? Am I sacrificing what I care about, putting myself second, for a purely financial benefit? In this case, my gut feeling might be that of a strong yes. The business has a good reputation and a strong base of existing clients which gives my gut a sense of emotional stability and no reason to worry. The sexual centre is also a yes and excited about the possibilities the cash is likely to unlock for my growing business. Perhaps I feel this as sexual excitement, or perhaps just as a warm glow or subtle movement of energy in my pelvic area.

In this particular case, three parts of my inner community are misaligned with one (the heart) which isn't convinced taking out a business cashflow loan is a good idea. This is a call to listen to the heart centre more closely and also to ask what reassurances/ other conditions it would need in order for its decision to also be yes. It's possible the loan can be arranged in a way my personal financial security isn't compromised. Or perhaps there are other forms of financing? Maybe it is enough to discuss this openly with my husband and strengthen our connection in agreeing to face this together and openly, if it becomes a problem. When a final decision is made it often feels like a compromise where a part or two of my inner community had their reservations, which were acknowledged. With complex decisions, there is rarely a strong "yes" on all levels. In my experience, what makes all the difference is letting the subtler voices within me have their say. And also, at least trying to meet the needs of the parts of me which are less often heard.

As I sit more with the topic of shame, I also realise how connected this is to my letting go, slowly but surely, of responsibilities in – and attachment to – my business. First, I let go of doing sales, which I used to excel at, and did continuously for more than six years. I had a very clear sense of value-add and satisfaction while I was bringing in the big deals. To a degree, the business relied on my doing what I did exceptionally well, and that felt great. Then I let go of a vision (coming mostly from my head and strong ego, I now realise) of launching a different branch of the business that would help other companies to implement aspects of open culture, such as our recruitment process, open salary, and more. The interest was there, I had had countless coffees and lunches with founders who wanted to pick my brains on how to do what we do. But the timing and the energy I wanted to birth this from weren't right.

Then, during a significant dive into my personal darkness, I decided to work only three days a week, and gave myself permission to travel pretty much wherever my heart wanted me to, and to work more than 50% of the time away from the office.

I see and feel that while the company operates in a way which gives people a significant amount of freedom to work wherever and whenever they want to, I have created a place in the world for myself where I can live almost entirely in freedom (apart from that which still binds me on the inside). Most people, in and outside of my company, don't live in complete freedom, and because I do, I sometimes feel shame. I feel shame because I choose myself and also because I have choices not many others do. I feel shame because somewhere inside me there's a place that's been taught that I don't deserve this, even though I also know that it is only by choosing myself first that I can truly be of service to the world, through all of my gifts and my brilliance. It is painful to realise that it still stings to choose myself, but it's true.

I have a lot of respect for founders, some of whom I know, who choose to leave their businesses, particularly when they are on the cusp of great success, and follow the call of the soul, over the call of responsibility and obligation. Often this means starting something else, as was the case with a friend, Anisah Osman Britton, who started 23 Code Street, teaching women to code, at a price in the UK, and for free in India. Sometimes it means dropping your past life and super successful career altogether, like another friend, Yaniv Charlap, to throw yourself into the unknown, travel the world, see where the Flow wants to guide you. In his case, a small island off the coast of Brazil where he purchased land from an old lady called Rosemary, and started an empowerment-focused community under the same name (rosemarydream.com). It takes guts to birth something and let it go knowing that it's likely to change, perhaps completely, compared to your initial vision. It will take on a life of its own which may have not much to do with the life you'd have wanted for it.

# Ready To Shine

One of the things strippers are unquestionably the best at is unapologetically shining their light, brilliance and charisma, regardless of age, gender, race or body shape. Unveiling not just the naked flesh but the inner shine is their job and this is why it's so difficult to get your eyes off a great stripper – their light becomes contagious. Since I've already spoken about the inner darkness, I also want to speak about the light, for one cannot exist without the other. And owning both is crucial in the context of entrepreneurship. Moreover, I would like to talk about "fitting out" (rather than fitting in) which is a familiar concept for strippers. It's all about refusing to be "normal". The more ridiculous your outfit or stage gags, the more you cleverly challenge political correctness, the better.

I remember an excellent act by a performer known as Audacity Chutzpah in which she skilfully acted out key events in the twentieth century to do with the emancipation of women. There was a woman flying a plane, a woman who just received the right to vote, a businesswoman with an amusing brick-like mobile phone from the eighties. With each new iteration of an empowered woman, Audacity progressively lost items of clothing, finally to remain only in her underwear, portraying a drunken young woman on a night out. To finish off the act, she unrolled a banner spelling out "LIBERATED" which made sense given the story the act told. Just before the music ended and it was time for her to bow, Audacity unrolled the remaining few centimetres of the banner with a question mark on it, introducing an unexpected twist, particularly in the context of an alcohol fuelled cabaret and burlesque night. Is stripping off in front of strangers, however glamorously, truly a sign of emancipation? Most people present (and the performers!) would definitely say so. Needless to say, Audacity Chutzpah definitely wasn't afraid of fitting out.

From a very early age, we absorb the message that it's not okay to stick out. If you try, you get bashed on the head by your peers (or an adult in charge) and swiftly brought down to "your level". Whether you stand out because you've mastered the system, or because you've refused to engage with it altogether, or even, tragically, just because you've tried something new and it failed, you are in trouble. And that's how it goes on, through puberty and adult life. As a society, we often, and unconsciously, push each other down like crabs trying to get out of a bucket. (Even though a bunch of crabs is more than capable of getting out of a container by forming a little ladder from their bodies, they aren't able to overcome an impulse to push each other down.) Many corporate environments are designed particularly well to enable the pushing down through restricted access to information, gender, racial and social prejudice, and an abundance of political games. We're once again in a territory of distorted, insecure and terrified masculine, as opposed to the essence of the masculine principle, which believes in brotherhood and working together towards a bigger goal.

Obviously, this is not the way it has to be. We can all rise together. In a way, we are not able to rise apart from one another, not sustainably. Every time I'm overcome by ambition, or fear, and focus on pursuing my path independently, I get reminded that this is not how it works. Whether it's about my personal healing, or professional success, in the bigger scheme of things I can't do it alone. And also, I don't exist in separation from the ecosystem around me, and if I feel that way, I usually haven't been sharing my talents and energy enough within communities I'm already part of. If you feel you can't be "yourself" with people around you, I challenge you to search wider and find a community where you can. If it feels very different to the social circles you are used to and somewhat out of your comfort zone, it's a good sign you are on the right track.

These days, I'm part of at least two communities where people are committed to staying on the path of searching for their truth, each in their own way, even though we all use particular practices (meditation in connection, tantra and shamanism) that speak to us. When I'm going through a dark patch, I do have a tendency to pull away from being active in these communities, but because I know it well by now, I'm able to spot the signs that I'm alienating myself early and counteract them. I recognise that at the end of the day, I'm abandoning myself while trying to find an "independence" which in fact doesn't exist. None of us lives in complete independence from other people, from the social systems (although you probably could, somewhere very remote), and from the nature which we're a part of (you could not, no matter how hard you try).

Back to inner light. It takes awareness and courage to set yourself apart, not because you're "better" or fundamentally more evolved than those in your immediate surroundings, but as someone who has come to a place in life where their talents – and possible transmission to a wider world – become apparent, and they are ready to give themselves permission to go all in. Taking some perspective, I think it only makes perfect sense that doubts come, often and on many levels. They give you a chance to discern the authenticity of the calling and lean into any feelings that may come as a result of giving yourself permission to, well, shine.

I'm talking about this as it's my wish and my prayer that more people in the world give themselves permission to shine. This is, in fact, quite likely the only thing that could save this planet – more people standing in their power, unashamed, free. Thanks to the unabashed brilliance shining through some people that I know directly: artists, teachers, friends and colleagues, I'm ready to be with myself in this way. I thank them right now for showing me what it's like to be free. What it's like to fly on the wings of their own truth, truth which doesn't need defending, doesn't need to be showcased or even upheld. It stands on its own. Just like them, I desire to live in quiet celebration of my truth, every day, with every breath.

## My Inner Voice of Fear Says

I can feel an unmistakable sense of disgust. Essentially, how dare you?! How dare you think you can live outside of the constraints most are still subject to? Who do you think you are to talk about sexuality, spirituality and the nature of life as if you knew it all, as if you had no shame?! Look, feel, it's still here! Don't forget where you came from, now that you act all enlightened!

You will regret this. You will be cut down to your size again, sooner than you think. Bad times will come again, depression, madness, you will suffer more than before, you will be punished because of how highly you think of yourself! Because you're daring to reach for the stars, to pretend you can bathe in freedom as if you weren't just a prisoner of this life, a prisoner locked up in your vastly limited and limiting container of a body, in line with how you've felt for most of your life. Remember that... You. Are. Nothing.

## My Inner Woman Says

Wow. Paradoxically, this last sentence from the voice of fear gives me more relief than any piece of advice or comforting could ever do. Yes, in the bigger scheme of things I am indeed nothing. An insignificant spark in a gigantic fire, a microscopic water drop in a flood. And it feels great. And I love it. And that's fundamentally all I could ever wish for myself. To be a drop in a river of love. In the bigger scheme of things, nothing at all. Thank you, Big Fear. Thank you for speaking up and thank you for being my counterpart.

# Show Up For Your Calling

I will never forget how I felt after I performed my first burlesque act in front of a real audience, in a real, and legendary cabaret joint (Madame Jojo's in Soho, sadly and to the massive dismay of fans recently closed and sold to a property developer). It was called *Out of Office* and it played on the idea of a power hungry corporate executive who secretly craves to surrender. I was as ready as I could be after countless hours of rehearsing. I had a stunning, made-to-measure suit on, with a slight retro twist and slightly bigger than I'd normally wear, to accommodate an elaborate costume made of leather belts and chains (and even a dog collar with a ball gag!) carefully hidden underneath the suit.

Everything was just perfect. My hair was slick and tied to the back. I had leather gloves and a leather bag I tossed on the floor as soon as I got on stage. In the act I'd just come back from a busy day at work, lounged on a sofa and made a quick pretend phone call to tell someone I was firing him for not getting good enough results on the sales team (he'd just had a baby which impacted his performance but who was I to care). I then started singing to the tune of *Why Don't You Do Right* famously performed by Jessica Rabbit in *Who Framed Roger Rabbit*. I changed the lyrics though which started with "I've had my way since the age of 23/I wrap men 'round my finger, they are fools for me."

As the act went on I could feel the electricity between me and the audience. Their full attention was completely on me, nothing else mattered in that moment. And I felt like a pure channel of fire, light flowing through me. As soon as I was finished I just knew I completely and utterly nailed it. Not because of the applause, which was super generous. It was an inner knowing: I had managed to enter a state of complete flow in the moment, to the point that I barely knew what was happening. I had absolute trust in every action and movement that came to me. And when

I was done I felt completely elated. I've never taken heroin, and don't intend to, but I imagine that's what the first hit might feel like. It's only that our bodies are perfectly capable of getting there naturally, when we stumble on what we truly love doing. In that moment, I knew that being in front of audiences, as a performer and also as a speaker, was my calling, and it brought the kind of aliveness I couldn't possibly experience elsewhere. And it was my conscious decision to act on what called me all those months ago to give a burlesque course a try, that got me there.

While my key interest in this book is an exploration of leadership from the feminine perspective, there's a time and place where the masculine (or animus, using Jungian language) needs to take the reins. In its nature, the feminine part, or anima, is passive as opposed to dynamic. It is its male counterpart that's an agent for change, restless where she is restful. That's why in his lectures spiritual teacher Osho recommends employing the animus to grow, and the anima to make your growth an established fact, to embed it in your very being.

In connection with this, there's fire in me, and even judgement, directed towards those who feel a calling, particularly around changing the world of work, but don't show up for it. Or don't show up for it in a way which is pragmatic, tangible, courageous and well-thought through (read: coming from the masculine principle within them). Some would say they have a talent for envisioning but not for delivering things. Personally, I don't trust that. We all have a capacity to do both, it's just that often we grant one side (in this case the feminine) more room to exist within us than the other (in this case the masculine). Note: delivering doesn't always mean rolling up your sleeves to do everything that needs to be done by yourself. It can mean getting together a team and resources, attracting the right sponsors and supporters. It means manifesting something in the material world and there are a thousand ways of doing so.

In the world we've built, on the planet we've been granted, the feminine principle cannot and will not rise without the support, and the grounding, of the masculine principle. If the feminine is a deep lake with hidden currents, the masculine is the banks around it. If the masculine is the agent of change, the feminine embeds and sustains that change. I see examples of this every day. A vision that doesn't become manifested in the material world is worth next to nothing in terms of its potential to transform the reality we live in. As they say in startup circles, ideas are cheap, execution is everything.

An entrepreneurial idea not backed by a strong masculine leadership which can help deliver on it turns into a mirage, a romantic longing but hardly anything more. I'm speaking to a lot of entrepreneurs I've met on my way, and to myself, also, here. There are definitely projects and ideas waiting to be born through me but in one way or another I'm not ready to let them live. Mostly because the fear and imposter syndrome kick in: who am I to make Project A happen in the world? Surely there's someone better equipped or qualified. And sometimes, I delay out of sheer laziness or wanting to stay in a bubble of relative comfort. It takes commitment, disciplined channelling of energy and a potential heartbreak waiting to happen in order to birth anything that has any significance.

Depending on where I'm at in life, the creative power of this kind doesn't always feel available to me but when it is, and I choose to ignore the call, sooner or later I feel a contraction, a blockage of my life force and generally a diminished sense of trust in myself. This can also manifest as lack of freedom and/or authentic self-expression in my life that I desire above all else. In essence, it's entirely up to me – and you – to follow the calls that life offers us. There are endless opportunities to create the kind of reality, and the kind of life, which you desire. And regardless of your gender, your inner man is here to help you.

# Getting Off Stage Gracefully (Or: Welcome To The Funeral Of Your Dreams)

To deliver a truly fabulous performance, the artist cannot just rely on the impression she or he made in the first ten seconds of the act, and not even on whether the performance is well put together and executed. The ending of it is just as crucial – is it well timed, does it make sense in the context of the story, does it leave the audience hungry for more? It's usually the ending of an act, the *grand final*, that leaves the most lasting impression. Similarly, a lot can also be said about the timely ending of a performer's career. After about two years of being an active burlesque artist, I lost the initial passion I felt for performing. Most of the acts I'd developed didn't feel congruent with my new interests. And so I decided to stop (not necessarily forever) instead of doing what was no longer entirely "me" as an artist, for financial or other reasons. It was a good exit, and if I ever wanted to come back to performing, I should be able to fairly easily find my way back onto the stage.

Time to talk about the opposite end of the spectrum, also connected to exercising the masculine part of your leadership: giving up when it's time to give up. Very often our biggest heartbreaks as founders involve letting go of our visions and dreams. Accepting that for whatever reason you haven't predicted, it's simply not meant to be. It's something so difficult to do, that many people simply avoid it. And so they remain in companies which never really get off the ground for a long time. It's sad to watch but at the same time I don't feel it's up to me to coach anyone on when it's an appropriate time to quit a vision (unless they specifically request that). It's up to all of us to learn, as one of the essential life skills, I feel, what is enough and where to draw the line in a given set of circumstances.

There's also a different way of letting go, in the case of a founder whose company has outgrown them. I began having that sense about a year or so ago. On one level it came as a realisation that I'm no longer needed to a degree I used to be, which felt both relieving (and worth celebrating!) and sad at the same time. On another level, I had a sense of how limited I actually am, as a person in a body and with a very particular set of skills. I am nowhere near enough to take this company where it wants to go, which is in many cases beyond what I envisioned, on a personal level. Coming to the realisation that it's time to put a such a deeply personal project to bed can feel like a funeral of your dreams. It's not easy to acknowledge that reality is way more complex and multifaceted than your vision. Sometimes, it's not the idea itself, but a particular way of executing it that simply isn't right. It may then become a question of whether your dreams are spacious enough to accommodate reality, as opposed to the other way round.

What is a funeral anyhow? It certainly has a very serious ring to it, in our cultural tradition. And yet, it can be a time and place of relief and lightness, as much as one of grief, depending on perspective. Some spiritual traditions and communities dance and sing during funerals to celebrate a soul's return to the Mother, as well as the beauty of the life just completed. After all, it is a sacred rite of passage, possibly the most important one for any individual human being. Passage from separateness back into Oneness. From substantial to insubstantial, subtle, and free. It's also the time to acknowledge all the awesome things that somebody (or a venture) was in their lifetime on this Earth. Personally, I would love to have a cracking blues band at my funeral, and a free bar (ideally with plant-medicine-based shamanic cocktails) for everyone to enjoy, commemorating my life and whatever the connection with me meant, and still means, for their own being. Can it brighten or inspire their own life, which is still burning and ready to bring them a new surprise in every moment, in some way? I'd certainly wish so.

And so, when it feels like one of your dreams needs a funeral, I'd recommend to process the feelings of sadness, resentment and bitterness first (if there are any), and then to ask yourself what you can celebrate. It can actually be exciting to let go of a part of you that you were so committed to, and to throw yourself into the arms of the Unknown. Clean again, free again. Waiting for what is to come now that you've recommitted your life, talents and powers to something much bigger, which knows and sees more than you could ever dream of. How beautiful to be in this flight, like a circus performer between one trapeze and another. Trusting but not quite knowing that the forthcoming bar will be there, at precisely the right time, for their now empty hands to grasp on to.

I also take the "funeral time" to look at what happened, to acknowledge and honour it all: the love, the blood, sweat and tears I've put into creating something new in the world, no matter if it ended up growing from seed and into a tree, or never even encountered a fertile ground. When I'm truly committed to something, it's naturally quite difficult to detach myself sufficiently to look at what I'm doing, and what I've achieved so far, from a higher perspective. When completion (or detachment, or funeral) time comes, everything aligns so that I can acknowledge both my positive impact and my weakness. This time to reflect on things I've done from a position of decreased attachment makes them, in my world, more meaningful. It doesn't make sense for me to throw myself into a string of new activities unless I can fully feel into that which I'm leaving behind first. One of my favourite authors, Clarissa Pinkola Estés, known best for *Women Who Run With The Wolves*, talks about the importance of creating *descansos*, so-called resting places for the parts of us that were on the way somewhere that they never got to. They become the markers of our dark times but also, as Estés points out, love notes to our suffering, a place to put down disappointment and rage so that something new can be born.

# Couples In Business

When in your stripper identity you are (obviously) always single and available, perhaps apart from double acts where it's clear the couple are also together in real life (but those are rare). I remember one such act where the man was a bodybuilder and threw his petite (and extremely hot!) partner up in the air to the awe and amazement of the audience. In all other cases though, from the punters' perspective, engaging with a stripper is all about the dance between accessibility (they get to see and experience more of you than ordinary bread eaters) and non-accessibility (they can't touch you or meet you afterwards for a date, unless they're really, really lucky!). You are so available on one hand, and so distant on the other. And if you have a partner, male or female, they must remain shrouded in mystery (unless they're Dita von Teese's infamous ex Marilyn Manson).

Interestingly, based on my experience at least, being in business with your life partner can also present challenges in terms of public perception. In the early days of GrantTree, I used to try and hide the fact I was in business with my then boyfriend, now husband, mostly out of shame and for the fear our little consultancy would be branded as a "mom and pop shop" (even though we aren't parents). In one instance, I'll never forget, for how embarrassed and angry I felt at the time, Daniel and I did really well putting up a "professional facade" in front of one of our first prospects. It was paramount to get their business – we were very early stage and not exactly swimming in cash. I was the commercial girl, he was the technical guy; we worked well together. Nobody needed to know we were together in life. In this particular meeting, the new client was ready to finally sign the contract and we were excited. Everything went well, we handled all the objections they raised with flying colours, it was time to sign and, perhaps, have lunch together to celebrate.

Once all the contract-related questions were out of the way, the client asked which particular networking activities I found helpful from the business development perspective. I attended loads and, in fact, met the person who was about to sign with us while out and about networking. I mentioned a particular event, which started before 7am in the morning over breakfast. I used to do several of those every week and worked hard to get business referrals for people from other professions around the table. I'll never forget how Daniel, having let his guard down for just a second, smiled from the corner of his mouth and uttered something along the lines of, "The annoying thing for me is that I usually drive her to those meetings." There was an awkward pause as it became clear we weren't just spending the working days together. The client decided he needed a little bit more time to ponder on the contract after all. In the end, after lots of chasing on my part, he said thanks but no thanks.

Obviously, we brought this on ourselves by being dishonest in our appearances to begin with. Would it have mattered to the client if they knew from the beginning that we were a couple? Probably not. We made it matter though by deliberately hiding that fact, and then letting it slip that the reality was different than the appearances. Still, our fears of "coming out" to clients in the early stages of our business weren't completely unfounded. There was and there still is, I feel, a stigma attached to couples being in business together. I've come across investors in tech startups, for example, who have a rule not to invest in companies run by couples, out of the assumption that if the relationship breaks down, so will the business. Personally, I don't see a pattern of companies run by couples being more likely to fail as a result of relationship breakdown between founders, as compared to startups run by two or three friends, or people who did not have a relationship of any kind before getting into business together. Statistics show that founder conflict is one of the top reasons for startup failure, regardless of what the pre-existing relationship might be between the founders.

For a few years now, we've paid little attention to external perceptions of our personal relationship while being in business together. Arguably, it's easier, of course, as the business is well established, with many other people in it. These days, we rarely attend the same meetings anyway. Still, when it naturally comes up that we're married, we have no problem with mentioning it and even answering questions about it. We've been more concerned about protecting our boundaries in terms of spending time together as a couple, and not founders. We once did a spontaneous exercise where we recalled one or two things that happened in each of the ten years we've spent together. Most of those things were to do with the company, how well it did, what crisis it went through, what challenges we faced. It was a little scary to realise most of our life together was built around being founders. These days we strive to have experiences and create memories that aren't connected to the company. It's become a lot easier since Daniel chose to retire in late 2019 and I started working part time.

If you're looking to start a business as a couple, don't let others (who just can't picture themselves working alongside their partner) persuade you that it will be a disaster. Just be realistic in terms of the impact it's definitely going to have on your relationship. This isn't to say couples that don't work together have an easier or a better life together. It's simply that being in business together will definitely transform the partnership in all sorts of ways, some of which are impossible to predict.

"Is it worth it?", some people ask me. It's a weird question and it very much depends on what the alternative is, which we will never know as we can't turn back time. For us, starting a business together was an important step we chose to take. We would be a different couple had we not taken it. I'm happy because of what now exists in the world because we put plenty of energy, time and effort into building it. I'm also sad as we gave up on lots of opportunities to be together in different ways, build intimacy as a couple, and grow in a different direction. A lot of the time, being founders kept us from being lovers. It also kept us distracted enough not to clearly see our challenges in how we relate to each other. On the other hand, it earned us financial freedom and plenty of creative satisfaction. It gave us the freedom to step away from the business. All in all, we can only know the path we've chosen together and I'm glad to be on it to experience what it brings.

# The Whore In Business

Many a burlesque act bring up the persona of a naughty office girl or a corporate dominatrix. In my first act, *Out of Office*, I reversed this stereotype, revealing my vamp's true and hidden desire to be used as a sex slave by the very men she bullies during the working day. No matter the type of character created by a burlesque artist, understandably a lot of acts feed on the taboo concerning all things sexual in the context of office-based work. This is taken to an extreme in American working culture, where a compliment on a woman's good looks could these days end in court on grounds of sexual harassment. While all women – and men! – should feel safe at work and in all other areas of life, I'm convinced that denying and repressing sexuality in any context sooner or later will result in a distortion, which itself is often hidden and, because of this, way more dangerous.

It is for this very reason that the International School of Temple Arts, where I trained in tantra, a philosophy and a path of life combining esoteric traditions of Hinduism and Buddhism, has an open approach to sexual interactions arising between teachers and students. Such interactions are allowed as long as there's awareness of the potential shadow aspects of such an interaction (e.g. attraction to perceived power or status) and plenty of peer-to-peer feedback before and as the connection unfolds. Understandably, this is seen by many as very controversial. I believe that it's overall much better that these connections happen in the light, and are open to scrutiny from every direction, as opposed to taking place in secrecy, which is often the case in other tantra and sexual healing oriented organisations.

And so, I want to talk about the feminine sexual energy and the way it can and does manifest itself in the office, not just on a burlesque stage. In fact, I wish we could welcome it more as a source of creativity and personal power. After all Eros is synonymous with, and inseparable from, Life Force energy. It can be manifested in all sorts of ways and I'm glad that in our office we've broken the taboo surrounding all things sexual and generally talk openly about relationships and sexuality, whenever it's consensual to bring up this topic of course. I'll never forget a male colleague asking openly on the company-wide Slack channel for recommendations of an appropriate central London establishment for a break-up conversation. Another colleague replied that it all depends on how long the relationship had been going for, presenting a range of potentially suitable options.

Personally, known for my politically incorrect love of filth around the office, I once received a birthday cake with shapely red letters forming the word CUNT on top of it. I was thrilled and remember prancing around the office, offering pieces of my cunt cake freely to whoever was keen. The Shoreditch bakery who created the masterpiece never forgot the unusual order and we became the local urban legend of the moment, to the point where when another colleague went to the same bakery to order a cake for someone else, more conventional this time, an excited member of staff shared, "You wouldn't believe it but some startup recently ordered a cake with CUNT written on it." "Yes, that was us," our colleague replied.

Based on my experience, and our cultural conditioning, our feminine counterparts are more deprived of openly expressing our sexual nature than our masculine counterparts. In the Western civilisation in the past hundreds of years, the Virgin archetype has squashed, diminished, and surrounded with shame the archetype of the Whore. An important narrative in our collective consciousness is that of a woman who is worthy and noble, a mother of a fabulous man (ideally: God Himself), while also remaining prudent and in control/suppression of her sexual energy (ideally – you've guessed it! – a virgin). Not exactly a straightforward path of leadership for the rest of us to follow.

The feminine globally is reclaiming her Eros, which translates to the roots of her embodied personal power. Importantly, according to the teachings of tantra, Eros doesn't equal sexuality but is intricately connected to it. I don't think I need to elaborate on the significance of embodied personal power in business. When we see and feel it, we know it. It's far from imposing or overwhelming. It's quietly self-assured but without the need to be right. It's radiant and feels empowering to those who find themselves in its vicinity. It has nothing to prove, often not even much to say. It brings a solid presence that acts in the world in a very precise manner and only when it needs to. I would like to see more women and men embody this power in my lifetime, and I know that I will.

An empowered and embodied woman – in other words one who has integrated her Whore (meant as an archetype) – is a considerable force in the world of work. Particularly if it's also a woman whose masculine qualities are well evolved, way beyond the distortion of the masculine that ultra-competitive and non-inclusive environments can encourage. I always look up to such women, whether their inner power and feminine-masculine balance is a result of a long journey of self-discovery or comes relatively naturally at an early age.

A close friend of mine, and a founder of a communications company, identifies and presents as a gay woman even though she's always felt her inner man somewhat stronger than her inner woman. It gives me joy to observe how the inner marriage works and manifests itself in her case. She is courageous, solid, reliable, practical and goal-oriented in the way some men I look up to in my life have been. At the same time she is graceful, empathetic and very aware of her personal values and the global impact she's aiming to have in her industry. It's a joy to be around her, when I can keep up with her vision and the speed at which she thinks (which I often can't!).

# The Courage To Feel

Quite a lot of people consider me courageous. When they say it, more often than not, they think about crazy things I've done, such as moving to the UK from Poland in 2006, stripping on stage, successfully pitching myself as a UK Country Manager to several Polish software companies two years later with precisely zero experience in business, no cock between my legs (which generally makes moving around in the technology industry easier) and a relatively thick Eastern European accent. Then I left an experienced business partner, almost thirty years my senior, and decided to start a company, on my own if I needed to. The honour of being the co-founder went to my boyfriend of a year who wasn't even enthusiastic about the business at first, as he was still mourning the failure of his previous venture. Before the second company was born, I even survived one year in London (room rent included, no support from parents, no debts incurred) on the sum of £10,000. The list goes on.

These aren't things I consider particularly courageous, even though I'm grateful to myself that I chose to go full in as the opportunities presented themselves. However, I will readily admit that alongside perseverance, which is definitely a trait I possess, I had a bit of fool's luck and early starter's chutzpah, combined with virtually nothing to lose. I can still do outrageous things today and derive some satisfaction from it. There's definitely more to lose these days but I also have the awareness that at the end of the day I don't really own anything – such as resources, money, health, talents, my life even – that wasn't given, for a while, and at some point will be taken away. However, I do find myself courageous, for different reasons. If you have a direct or indirect experience of what tends to be branded as "mental health difficulties" (and research shows that at least a third of us do), you may be able to identify with the below, or find it interesting.

As I began to work less and have the capability to spend more time with myself, I chose to simply be, as opposed to continue to define myself through what I did or managed to accomplish. This brought on some pain, fear and confusion which I wasn't ready to face and had been keeping at bay for years, mostly through relentless productivity. Am I ready to face it all now? I'm not entirely sure one ever is. What I am sure of is that the longing for lost pieces of myself seems greater than the worry of what I must face on the way to find them. From then on, it's a plunge into the unknown.

From what I know so far, the unclaimed part of me involves sensitivity beyond measure and ability to feel the pain of every even slightly self-judgemental thought I have, and the slightest perceived ignorance in the world around me. It also involves excruciating, childlike confusion about it all, and the meaning of simply being in my body in this world. There's the pain of not belonging here at all, unless I work super hard to earn that right. There's desperately wanting to be seen in all that I am and shame about that need (as a part of me believes I should be able to hold myself in everything that arises). There's the awareness of massive chaos that underpins all the neatly constructed social structures and all the parts of my identity I've built to protect me from it.

Why do I choose to go there at all, some of my friends wonder. I do it because otherwise I'll always feel like I'm choosing to run away from something vital and live in the shadow of that thing looming over me. Because having the courage to do this seems like the highest expression of love and respect towards myself, even if in the moments of a soul-crushing wave of terror I have no concept of what love is or if it really exists. I know many others are on this path because it feels meaningful to them, perhaps you are too. This gives me encouragement, although what keeps me going above all is the fundamental craving to meet myself.

And that's also why I, these days, hesitate to frame this journey as a struggle with "mental health difficulties". That would imply I have an illness, which for years I believed I did, as it gave me some comfort. Our conditioning seems to imply that unless we're happily productive throughout our lives, something must be wrong with us. Could craving and pursuing the truth about oneself be an instinct not to trust, though? Perhaps there's no "illness" in me that needs eradicating after all. And perhaps living life in a conscious way involves more courage than I'd ever need to do something outrageous.

I have the courage to feel. And, these days, I also have the courage to stop almost whatever I'm doing, and feel. I'm tired of putting pressure on myself to be productive, successful and socially immaculate *on top of* the fear that I feel. I long to meet myself on the other side of the backlog of things to process. I also notice that when I try to do several things at the same time, that which takes the most courage to do, and produces the least immediately visible results you can feel acknowledged for in the outer world, falls to the wayside. This is how I abandon myself. The more I do this, the lesser the chance I will ever find the courage to change the pattern. And, consequently, to bring the entirety of who I am back to my business.

Because of my experiences, I'm a massive advocate of supporting mental health and well-being in the business context. If you're a founder or a leader in a business, don't underestimate how much your influence as a mental health and wellness advocate can achieve, lives saved included. In practical terms, this translates to encouraging people to feel what they feel and to go through difficulties in life while being present with what's going on, even at the expense of work. There will always be work to do whereas, to pick a vivid situation some of my team experienced while working for us, you lose your father once. The way you are able to show up to support yourself and your family depends, to a meaningful degree, on how much freedom you have (including at work) to focus on the task at hand. Nothing quite as dramatic needs to happen though for someone to be in need of taking a break from regular activities or reducing their productivity.

A couple of years ago a member of the team went through a particularly difficult time while in psychotherapy and needed to take several months off work. Since then, we have secured a long-term sickness insurance that allows our team members to take longer amounts of time off for mental health or other health related reasons, if they need to. We also have a policy which allows anyone to take time off during the working day, to cope with anxiety, and people often use it. Are we worried that people might take advantage of it for illegitimate reasons? Not really. We trust them to manage their affairs, their energy and their workload because nobody else knows how to manage it better. In turn they seem to trust the company not just with their power but also with their vulnerability. I'll never forget an email a senior colleague sent to the whole team to communicate she'd split up with her long-term partner and so needed to reduce her output for a while and asked for the support of the team. It was very moving to see her trust and openness. She received an overwhelming amount of encouragement and offers of support in response. I know this is possible not just at GrantTree, but in many workplaces around the world. I choose to work towards the future where it will be possible everywhere.

To wrap up, I appreciate myself and all those of you who have the courage to feel. I appreciate people in my life for their presence and making it possible for me to feel things in connection with them. I appreciate the opportunity to know myself through them. And I use the power that I have, as an employer, to make it possible for others to be present for themselves.

# Do I Want To Hustle In This Joint? (Or: How To Interview A Company You're Potentially Interested In Working For)

Having been affiliated with a collective that aims to support professional strippers and to improve their working conditions, I'm very much aware of how awful those can be. I was shocked to discover that girls who work as lap dancers more often than not have to not only share their earnings with the club where they work but also pay an entry fee per night worked, regardless of whether or not they find any customers. On top of this, the club bosses often specify what the girls must wear and don't offer any of the support most other employers would do, such as maternity leave or sick pay. This is why a stripper must be aware of what they are stepping into and what their priorities are when entering into a contract with a club owner. What are they likely to earn? Will they be treated with trust and respect by both the management and the clientele? Will they be in control of what they wear on the job and in front of whom they perform? Will they have the freedom to decide when to take time off, even if unpaid (which is unfortunately usually the case in the stripping world)?

Some of the best candidates I interviewed for GrantTree (at the open culture interview stage) interviewed me straight back and, in some cases, fiercely. A really experienced candidate who works with us right now wanted to know how I could have answered the questions that I asked him and even how I might act in the challenging situations he described in his interview. He asked me what style of leadership I favour, and how I might choose between two conflicting perspectives, a question I posed to him only minutes earlier. I remember feeling a rush of adrenaline in my body and being very alive in this conversation. He truly cared to know whether what he'd read and heard about

GrantTree matched the reality. Who were the people he would be working alongside on a daily basis? What was their opinion of the culture and the company? I really value when candidates express their self-love and self-respect by wanting to know exactly what they're getting themselves into. Is what we talk about when we describe our culture just marketing? How do we really operate, and why? Why did I start this company to begin with and why do I still choose to work here, given I could start something else or be doing something entirely different?

Many people I interview assume I "work in HR" and so miss out on the opportunity to dig much deeper. Some have asked me how long I've worked at GT and some have checked my name on LinkedIn and so have realised I'm one of the founders, but not many. Most people are still essentially expecting to be told what to do within the recruitment context and don't have much interest in going beyond the traditional employer-potential employee dynamic, which is sad. Because at the end of the day, whether or not we choose to acknowledge it, underneath all the labels and roles we are simply two humans having a moment together which can be as deep and as truthful as we are prepared to go.

What are the questions I wished some of the candidates asked me? Probably why I choose to do what I do. What I feel when I do it. What I'm proud of and ashamed of, in the company I created. What I think it will take to manifest our vision. What their own impact could be, if there were no limits as to what they can achieve in the company (which, given someone who was hired as a client manager five years ago is now effectively the CEO, is largely true). And also, how to find a job where they can develop as people and actually stand and act in their power, regardless of whether or not they end up working for GrantTree.

There's so much more than can be done by the candidate, beyond speaking with me or one of my colleagues in the interview itself. These days many candidates investigate who we are as a company and apply because they're actively interested in working with us because of who we are. Some inquire even when we're not hiring for a position they'd be looking to fill, and stay in touch with us over a period of time. Quite naturally these people have a much higher chance of capturing our interest. Which isn't to say we select people purely on the basis of whether they're fans of what we do. In some ways it actually helps if they're not, and are happy to poke holes, in a productive way, in multiple areas of our business that still need to be disrupted, and to point out as and when we outgrow systems and structures that once represented a good solution to a particular problem.

# The Art Of Mutual Tease (Or: Conflict That Creates)

The most charismatic burlesque and fetish performances I've seen involve a story where, at least to begin with, something doesn't work. My own first act featured a businesswoman who "stomped on dead bodies of men on her way to the top" but actually secretly desired to be a sexual slave. My last – a woman fighting a man for the title of The Last Remaining Superhero of the Galaxy. In yet another one, with multiple and attention grabbing on-stage costume changes, I performed as an angry housewife, turned Catherine II Tsarina of Russia, turned female assassin, all on a mission to destroy men (in a comedic anger-driven way). This last act was particularly popular, and usually the audience's favourite, since it involved a good intrigue with a touch of self-irony. I performed it on various stages, including in Toronto, and more often than any other act I've ever created. I would emerge to a James Bond tune in a pink satin shower cap and an old robe (all the other layers of costumes hidden underneath!) angrily sweeping the stage. The song that followed, and which I sang live, was a standard very popular amongst burlesquers, *Fever*, for my purposes rebranded to *Cleaver*, with amended lyrics telling the stories of different female murderesses throughout the ages, in line with my outer appearance transforming. Every good story needs some form of drama and conflict to really engage the audience. Acts based on good stories tend to be the best. In a similar way, in business, teams that have gone through and survived a conflict (or two…) tend to be the most effective.

According to Diana Richardson, a teacher, author and practitioner of holistic body therapies (and a disciple of Osho), the masculine aspect, present within both genders, is the active energy, which can be compared with the feminine aspect using the following opposing qualities: yin/yang, moon/sun, night/

day, passive/dynamic. Leadership from the masculine principle therefore focuses on moving the needle, creating change, getting from A to B. Conversely, leadership from the feminine part is more concerned with what's the current reality, what's present right here right now. Where the masculine focuses on defining and executing a task, the feminine is more concerned with nourishing and harnessing a relationship (or, more likely, a set of relationships). A world where strong networks and relationships matter more than goals (as opposed to being a means to achieving goals) is where the feminine can flourish.

We live deeply embedded in relationships, in our personal and professional lives (whether or not we tend to draw a distinction between those). These relationships can, and often do, resemble a tennis match, borrowing the metaphor from Tom Kenyon, teacher, scientist, psychotherapist and sound healer. You aim to play with the best technique you have, using moves and tricks you know from your training and other matches that took place earlier. For some, it's more about getting the upper hand, never losing control over what's actually happening on the court. For others, it's more about the elegance, and the pleasure even, of the game itself. For most, there are matches of both kinds, depending on circumstances and the nature of sparring partners. But when all is said and done, a match is a match. There's a score and there's a goal, even if that goal is more about having a good game together than winning over your partner.

There's a different perspective on relationships I feel drawn to and even, at times, manage to implement. One where this "match" becomes more like a mutual tease or a dance that could lead absolutely anywhere, at any moment. When I think about this, the image that comes to mind is of a dance that continues even when the dance floor spontaneously disassembles and gravity vanishes. Why would this be a reason to stop dancing? Such a relationship often becomes a mirror for everything that you are. Which is also why, sooner or later, if you look closely enough, and for long enough, unless you are a Buddha-like perfectly enlightened being, you'll see something ugly in that mirror.

The really interesting thing is what you'll choose to do with what you saw. Of course, you can follow your first impulse, the one which tends to come after the pang of pain (or shame or resistance) is felt, and decide it has absolutely nothing to do with you. Surely, the person you are relating with has brought this into your world. All you need to do is to cut them off – physically or emotionally – and the pain will go away with them. Easy enough to do. You can also wait out the first impulse and feel into what's actually happening and what's being reflected back at you. This is when the possibility of expansion, that every relationship presents, truly opens up.

This makes me think of my relationship with an early team member and an ex-employee of GrantTree, I'll call him Tom. Tom and I were the biggest rainmakers on the team. We didn't muck about. We went after the big deals and we got them. I still remember being locked in a room together, making cold calls on loudspeaker, making silly faces at each other waiting for someone to answer on the other side. Singing along with the tune that played when we were getting put on hold while the office manager or the PA checked whether the Very Important Potential Decision Maker was currently "in a meeting" or not. We would take turns to speak with the prospects, on loudspeaker, while the other person was listening in, noiselessly making even more silly faces at the poor bastard trying to sell something from across the table. That was fun.

I personally brought Tom into the business. We were looking to expand the commercial side of our modest team of four (or five) and he was serendipitously introduced to me by a networking contact, why exactly I can't recall. He was on the lookout for a new project to get involved in and I quickly figured out that he was smart, eloquent, honest and that he could sell.

He had things in his first impressions toolkit which I, being an Eastern European girl with an accent, definitely did not, and that was great. I knew we needed what he had and so we made him an offer according to what we could afford at the time: lowest possible salary with a 20% commission on all business brought to GrantTree, with a multi-year commission agreement (meaning that when the client sold by a particular person stays with us over several projects, commission on that deal is still due for several years). But looking back, I also now know on a much deeper level why I actually brought Tom into the team, from a personal perspective. I had no way of knowing back then, obviously, what would unfold between us.

As months and years passed with Tom on the team, things gradually shifted between us. Looking back I can see a few reasons why which I wasn't able to at the time. First, he gave himself permission to step away from sales and relentless target hitting quite a bit earlier than I did, to get involved in other projects in the company that piqued his interest. That angered me, on a subconscious level, as I wanted the same for myself but the burden of responsibility for the team's commercial success I placed on myself was way too heavy and I wasn't able to give myself permission to let go of it, back then. Secondly, he decided to put together possibly the most financially ambitious – and risky – project to do with office space and property the company has ever undertaken. It ended up being a massive learning curve both for him and the company, with results and costs far from what was envisioned but, it has to be said, it was truly audacious. In other words, and it feels icky to say it even now, the kind of stuff I love to get stuck in, the big impossible, the risky but potentially game-changing kind of project. But I didn't. I was way too paralysed by my fears and perceived responsibilities towards the rest of the team and so I gave him my blessing to go ahead.

As our ways, in terms of day-to-day activities in the company, parted, there wasn't enough information about the project being publicised (as per what I expected), and unexpected costs kept mounting, my trust deteriorated. Things went out of control financially and the future started looking grim for the company for a while. I got wrapped up in a judgement of Tom, which I hadn't expressed for a while, for fear of confrontation. The way I saw it at the time is that everything I worked for was put at stake because of someone's personal ambition to complete an audacious project. I didn't stop to have an in-depth conversation about what I felt about the way things progressed though. Instead, I blamed myself and my co-founder for not having set up boundaries in such a way that this considerable mistake was impossible to make. We were so adamant to maintain people's freedom to work on things that interested them and were beneficial to the company, we overlooked the risks.

By the time Tom and I did have a conversation, or tried, it was too late. I'm sure Tom was aware of my lack of trust. In the end, the load of resentment that built up on both sides was so heavy, it seemed impossible to work through. At the time, I was in a fragile state because of other burdens I'd placed on myself, and Tom wasn't very used to talking about his feelings. He concluded it wasn't that important for us to work together since I was still in sales and so he was okay to simply liaise with Daniel. He actually said he didn't particularly respect me professionally (and least from what I understood) which was refreshing, although obviously painful, to hear. Nobody else I've ever worked with has ever had the guts to say it (even though I'm quite sure some people actually thought that) and so, from a longer perspective, I'm genuinely impressed and, in a way, grateful. But at the time, given I brought him to the company and we worked alongside each other for years, hearing that he didn't care enough about taking our relationship to a higher ground hurt so much, I wasn't able to process it and move on. The attempted conversation stopped and he soon left the company.

Tom remains one of the best mirrors, professionally, I have ever had. We reached out to each other, first me, then him, since he left, but we never actually met. I sense that we will, in the right time. Is there something I wish I'd done better? Of course and yet I recognise the situation took me beyond my capacity to handle a conflict given where I was at the time. Things played out the way they could at the time, to the end. At the end of the day, Tom was an aspect of me, as I was an aspect of him. It was too painful to stay in the light of the truth for both of us. Which I have compassion for even though the memories still bring emotion.

# Dealing With Hecklers (Or: Aspecting As Conflict Resolution Tool)

Pretty much all artists, whether performing or other, have an inner heckler. It's the part of us that firmly believes we will embarrass ourselves by bringing our creation to life and can cause a lot of damage. Mine would get active not merely when on stage (or just before getting on it) but almost inevitably halfway through the process of creating an act. If you like to create things yourself, you are likely to recognise this. When inspiration first strikes, you feel invincible. You are extremely excited and you know that once the idea is brought to life, the world is going to embrace it with open arms. For a burlesque artist, almost anything can bring about a concept for a new act or a new character. It can be a piece of music, a story heard somewhere, an encounter with someone new or a pair of vintage shoes that suddenly give them an idea for a costume. Work on a new piece begins. And suddenly, in comes the inner heckler. The heckler's agenda is to destroy the creator's trust in their creation and sadly, all too often, they manage to accomplish it. Having dealt with the heckler every time I work on something new, I now understand their presence as simply a part of the creative process. After an initial rush of adrenaline, there comes significant doubt as to whether the idea is worth anything. Very often, when this happens, I check in with a friend, just about anyone who wishes me well or, if I'm strong enough, I simply carry on knowing the heckler mustn't get to decide whether my idea will see the light of day or not.

Such was the case with *Big Blender*, an act I created to the tune of *Big Spender* (as you have probably figured out I have a thing for twisting classic tunes and turning them into something ridiculous). I was to have a real blender on stage and as I sang the song, I was to mix a cocktail live on stage, to share it with the audience at the end of the act. When I came up with the idea, I was overjoyed. Surely no one has stripped, sung a song and made a cocktail at the same time! Then, as I wrote the lyrics and started fleshing out the act itself it became evident that I wasn't going to be able to do all that I envisioned because of timing. For starters, the cocktail would have to be a pretend one. Suddenly, my neat idea started falling apart and with it my trust that the act was worth creating and performing. As I was part of a burlesque course, every one of us got to create an act by the end of six weeks and so, thankfully, and with plenty of encouragement from others, I persevered. In the end the act turned out to be witty, attention grabbing and very well received everywhere I got to perform it.

So much for the inner heckler. Things can get even more difficult when the heckler is another person though. There are many ways of approaching difficult conversations and conflict situations with people. At GrantTree some of us use non-violent communication methods, some choose to have a mediator when stepping into a meeting that is likely to be triggering. Giving and receiving difficult feedback is unequivocally the one skill consistently well-performing and self-managing teams must master. It also happens to be a fabulously useful life skill. The good news for those, like me, who still struggle to communicate masterfully in triggering situations, is that one can do quite a bit of work on one's own to be able to approach a difficult situation with groundedness and clarity.

I recently discovered my capacity to play different iterations of a possibly triggering conversation in my subconscious (while dreaming), and sometimes even in the conscious mind. By doing this, the field between me and the other person seems to clear so that when we meet, it feels as if the most difficult things have already been said and done – in my own head. This isn't always an easy process to conduct internally – particularly that you need to be able to abandon your perspective and step into the other person's shoes – but can be extremely useful.

For me it unfolded recently, and quite spontaneously, in connection with my mum. She was on my mind for days, and also in my dreams. But not in a serene way. We were fighting, the way only triggered mothers and daughters can. I would wake up not even remembering any of the content of what was said between us in my dreams, but with a clenched feeling of anger. The sort of anger which I would tend to have in an extremely triggering exchange with someone, one where I would keep hooking emotionally on to what is said, instead of letting it softly sink into the space between us. When my mum and I actually met, there was a sense of lightness in me, a sense of letting go of bearing responsibility for "playing it right". And it felt easy, surprisingly easy, to be together despite all the heavy stuff in my feminine lineage, which I'd been feeling through before.

If you'd like to play with this, here's an awesome exercise we do at ISTA, the mystery school I've mentioned before, called aspecting. It's, in a way, very simple, which is why you may feel discouraged to really go for it, as I did at first. And yet, it was one of the most powerful exercises of this type I've ever learnt. When you're ready to begin, sit on a pillow and imagine the person you need to talk to, sitting on another pillow opposite you. It could be someone you feel too scared or angry to approach at the office, someone you haven't spoken with in years or even someone who's passed away. As if they were really sitting opposite, simply tell them everything that must be said (or yelled) from your perspective, no censorship. Taking this into a business context, you could easily be talking to your co-founder, an annoying client or a member of staff you are experiencing problems with.

Once you feel you are empty, for now, sit on the pillow opposite and imagine looking back at yourself. I've even used a photograph of me for this at times. Feel into whatever this other person is likely to be feeling, given the impact of what was previously said by yourself to them. Very often, something surprising arises in the moment, quite different to what you thought this other person may feel or want to say, back when you sat on your own pillow. Sometimes you learn something you had no way of knowing but which is true for that person. For example, you learn something about their background or what motivated them to act in the way they did. It's an incredible feeling to get this sort of message.

Keep switching between the pillows until there's a sense of a resolution coming. This resolution doesn't look in a particular way. Some people find a compromise or a mutual understanding with their conversation partner, others end up embracing the other pillow and crying. However, if, for example, you were abused as a child and you are speaking with your abuser for the first time, this is very unlikely to be the outcome. What may happen instead is that there is more of a sense of neutrality, you seeing the other person and them being able to fully see you. It could be a neutral thanks and goodbye for now. It could be a thanks and goodbye forever as you discover there isn't, energetically and emotionally, a pathway for the two of you to get to a shared understanding, for whatever reason. You may end up with the other pillow pushed halfway across the room, away from you.

More often than not though, if you do this exercise with attentive presence both for yourself and for the other, something shifts between the two of you even though, practically speaking, your partner obviously wasn't actually there. But you have come out changed, or with a much wider perspective on the situation, and very often that's all that is needed.

This tool can easily be applied to those situations in business, involving other people, where you seem stuck, sometimes despite multiple attempts to set things right. It allows you to say all the things you'd normally find difficult to say or wouldn't want to, for the fear of aggravating the conflict instead of leading to its resolution. Often, as described above, an insight might come as to why the other person behaves the way they do, or how and why the way you behave impacts them. Sometimes simply going through this exercise lessens your own emotional charge and equips you to handle the situation in real life from a different, expanded perspective. Lastly, as a business leader you can use the tool to interact with different parts of you facing an important decision. For example, whether to enter into a lucrative business deal which raises some ethical concerns due to the business activities of the prospect. The aspecting exercise can then become a stage where different parts of you are invited to express their doubts, concerns and even get angry at each other.

# One Tease Too Far (Or: Conflict That Destroys)

Not all burlesque acts are fabulous and a pleasure to watch. Some are very clichéd, not really presenting or exploring anything new. Some have a poorly put together storyline, where, for example, the striptease part happens for no good reason and isn't preceded by a story which makes it a natural conclusion. Sometimes the music doesn't work for the act, at other times the costume or props seem not thought through well enough. Perhaps the most frustrating acts for the punters to watch though are those that involve lots of teasing but not much "action" – which could mean stripping but could also mean jokes or self-ironic gags on the part of the performer (a classic one here is taking off a stocking or a heel, smelling it and throwing it away in disgust). You can't sustain a good act on teasing only. It must lead somewhere and unfold, taking the audience on a journey with you.

Similarly to mistimed or badly-created acts, some conflicts in the business world are far from a fertile ground which nourishes the feminine part of your leadership capacity. They feel more like endless spin or a Gordian Knot (which, according to a Greek legend, Alexander the Great was tasked with untying, only to realise the best way of dealing with it was to cut right through it with his sword). One such example at GrantTree is the famous sales commission conversation, which comes up again and again even after all options have been discussed thoroughly and the conclusions made. From time to time someone in the sales team will raise the question: but why can't we implement some kind of commission structure? To which the remainder of the team rolls their eyes.

At the beginning of our commercial team expansion efforts, we had a disproportionately high commission coupled with a close to minimum salary, as that was the only model the company could afford at the time. This created a legacy of conflict and distrust between our commercial and delivery teams, which lasted long after the commissions were eradicated. The delivery team felt secondary and resentful towards the business because of it, for understandable reasons. They were taking home quite a bit less and their successes were celebrated much less than big contracts the sales team brought in. Salespeople argued that if it weren't for them, the business wouldn't exist. As a commercially-focused professional I actually very much identified with this myself – contracts and cash in are very much the lifeline of any commercial organisation. The trouble is, exactly the same could be said about the importance of the delivery team. In other words, what's the point of selling anything if it won't be delivered, and to a high enough standard, that clients are happy to pay for the work that we do and give us their business in the future? All that those pesky salespeople bring is unpredictable workload – cash only comes in after the delivery work, if the work has been done, and done well.

This conflict, which for all I know exists in most organisations (whether it's obvious or festering behind temporary fixes), is best illustrated by the tale about a salesperson and a developer who went bear hunting together. My other half and business partner Daniel liked it so much when he first heard it as a joke about salespeople in the developer circles, he published quite a popular article building on it. Since good artists copy and great artists steal, it feels like a good time for me to claim it! Warning: not suitable for vegans (however, no bears were hurt as part of the writing process).

*And so, once upon a time a salesgirl and a developer decided to hit the woods. Not just to have a quiet night under the stars though, these two were determined and not in it for idle play. The end game is, for some entrepreneurs, to retire, and spend their forties onwards being served piña coladas (or something similar) on a beach by suited waiters. It wasn't for these two. Following their primal calling and entrepreneurial ambition, they decided to bring their skills from the digitised world into a very real world and... to hunt some grizzlies. They took necessary tools and trekking gear with them and set off into the sunset. After some time, they came upon a clearing in the forest that felt good enough to set up a camp. The following day, the developer, being hands-on and practical, got down to the business of building a wooden shed to store their gear and hopefully, soon, some smoked bear meat. The salesgirl took off her colourful nail varnish (to blend in better in case grizzlies had good sight, she wasn't sure), packed an axe and a compass, left the iPhone behind (real salespeople focus 100% on the job at hand) and left the camp.*

*She was gone for days, so long that the developer, having finished building the hut, also finished the beer stash they brought with them, and also his own personal secret stash, and even checked whether it was possible to have a pizza delivered into a clearing in the woods. It wasn't. The hunger and the hangover got the better of him though and he started thinking about smashing the hut up and getting the hell out of the place. He thought that the salesgirl was likely flirting with some "prospect" on a golf course or at a posh pool party: these people didn't have much of a clue about what real work was anyhow.*

*When the developer was about to give in, he heard a rumble in the bushes on the other side of the clearing. Something was moving towards him! And, suddenly, there's the salesgirl, dirty and bruised, with hair all over the place and makeup smeared across her face, running towards him like he's never seen her run before. The determination in her eyes, that is quite something. The smell of adrenaline of a nearly-closed deal in the air. Seeing her like this, teetering on the edge of glory with a victory flag unfurled, the developer has a flash of understanding exactly why she does what she does.*

*She's nearly at the hut when she shouts "Get OUT! Open the door!!" in a way it's impossible to disobey. A few seconds later – yes, it's true! – a bear tumbles across the clearing too, chasing her. "What a beast!" thinks the developer. "This thing could honestly feed a village.*

*If only there was anyone out there brave enough to kill the damn thing."
And then, in a split second, the salesgirl's plan becomes obvious. As
she runs towards the door of the shed, she seems to be leading the bear
directly into it. Just as she is about to burst through the door, she skips
to the side but the bear isn't quick enough to follow. Full force, he
barges in, and the salesgirl swiftly closes the door shut behind him and
bolts it. Terrifying crashes are soon heard from inside of the shed, as the
bear trashes everything he can reach, desperately trying to find a way
out in the darkness. The salesgirl wipes the sweat, and the eyeliner, off
her forehead and looks over at the developer. "Wasn't that neat?" she
says. "I'm getting kinda bored here though so why don't you go and
skin him while I'm off to the other edge of the forest to find us a second
one."*

Developers often hate salespeople and vice versa. Salespeople
hate marketing people and vice versa. Those conflicts have, more
often than not, absolutely nothing creative to offer. They stem
from a useful difference of perspectives, but without a genuine
effort on both sides to find out the truth of a given situation. In
my experience at least, they often arise because one or both sides
are too lazy, or simply unwilling, to abandon their own stance in
order to look at the problem from someone else's point of view.
Sometimes it's a matter of immaturity, sometimes a matter of
overwhelming attachment to your own way of seeing the world
and making sense of what you see. The way to deal with these
kinds of conflicts is, in my opinion, to not go there to begin with,
unless you're willing to challenge yourself and/or others out of
mental and emotional stuckness.

If a conflict you chose to bypass keeps coming up, let it
simply be in the collective field. The more you fight it, the more
space it's likely to take. If you let it be (even though you know it
leads nowhere), more often than not, soon enough the attention
of those involved will shift to something else as the internal and
external reality of your business unfolds.

In theory, the matter of whether we should reintroduce

commissions at GrantTree is something as a team we could choose not to entertain again. However, it would jeopardise the freedom of speech and expression that we value more than the nuisance of having to explore the same arguments over and over again. Conflict between teams can be really destructive to any company. If it's handled well it can contribute to the team's unity. However, most definitely not all conflicts are constructive and worth leaning into, in terms of full emotional engagement. Sometimes setting things up structurally in a way that prevents ongoing disharmony from happening is the best solution, as my co-founder and I felt was the case with commissions in our company. We are well aware of the risks to do with potentially discouraging a pool of strong candidates from applying to work with us. Still, we favour incentive structures seeking to reward the entire team, as opposed to particular parts of it, also as an investment in the company culture.

# The Art Of Revelling In Pain

What I really want to talk about in this chapter is your inner feminine leader's capacity of staying in a place that hurts instead of swiftly turning away from discomfort. While I wouldn't say I'm a dedicated fetishist, my brief romance with fetish modelling while I was an active showgirl helped me develop a skill of observing discomfort with curiosity, and also as an artistic medium. Clearly, some people get there with days, weeks and months of silent meditation, whilst others... while exploring their inner sadomasochistic exhibitionist in front of the camera!

Back when I did, I developed a friendship with a professional photographer in his sixties who, as he confided in me once, was getting bored with "normal" (in his world!) burlesque and boudoir shoots and loved experimenting for example with the Japanese bondage art called Shibari, which – provided one is a good rigger, which he was – lends itself very well to dark, artistic, and often erotic, photography. There were two photoshoots with my older friend which I remember particularly well. First, because for days afterwards I had a small burn on my belly, having placed ten wax candles all over my body in his darkened studio. Second, because it was the most physically challenging shoot I've ever done (okay, perhaps next to posing in a black bikini in a beautiful old cemetery in the middle of December) and that was when I learnt the true meaning of physical surrender. In the middle of my friend's studio, he used his considerable Shibari skills to create a massive "spider web" in the middle of which was I, bound up and – at least for the duration of the actual shoot – fully suspended from the ceiling. Whilst being completely incapacitated – at one point the photographer had to climb up a ladder to feed me a little water to drink – I felt exceptionally alive. I knew it would only take his inexplicable decision to leave me fully suspended for a little longer than required for me to pass out. My life was completely in his hands in that moment. I remember feeling numb in my wrists, with rope tied tight around them, and quite lightheaded (hence the necessity of the manoeuvre of feeding me water from the ladder). I was very uncomfortable and yet totally revelling in the discomfort. When I was actually fully suspended, I remember concentrating on my breathing, terrified at the thought of how embarrassing – and impractical – it would have been if I actually fainted.

Still, the capacity of staying in a place that hurts emotionally is definitely one that I, within the feminine part of my leadership, am still mastering. The place of discomfort and even what sometimes feels like pure emotional torment, approached from the right perspective, often becomes a birthplace of power and freedom. When you're in the middle of it though it's, of course, next to impossible to believe. And so we look for a way out, or a particular framing of the situation so that someone or something is to blame for the discomfort that we feel.

Three years into the existence of GrantTree, one of my best friends at the time joined the sales team. We were so close she offered to organise my hen do on the island of Gozo (near Malta) which was a lot of fun. This made it all the more surprising for Dan and me to discover, not long after our wedding, the friend had been starting a directly competitive business on the side, and signing up clients on GrantTree work time, using our marketing materials, while under a full employment contract with us. There were two other people involved in the venture but one of them had second thoughts – perhaps because of the substantial professional and personal help we had given them in the past – and decided to tell us what had happened.

Quite understandably, we were both heartbroken. This felt like a stab in the back, particularly given that we were already, at the time, committed to fostering a culture of respect, trust and honesty. We had zero experience of dealing with such an issue, so we asked our employment lawyer, who came up with a legal case and a formal investigation plan, including evidence gathered thus far, which we presented to the people in question. During the first part of the investigation, the rest of the team couldn't be informed about what was actually going on, for legal reasons, which demanded a lot of trust from them. What happened was extremely painful, and we didn't know better than to take strict measures to protect the company immediately. But there was something else at play also. We weren't able to stay in the utter discomfort of this situation without framing it in a particular way. Someone needed to be made wrong and in this case, as those who hear this story tend to agree, my close friend and her collaborators were the deeply unethical ones, and so the choice was easy. Could there have been other ways of looking at the event and subsequently dealing with it? Absolutely.

The first question really worth asking was: why did this situation arise in the first place? Yes, there was personal greed at play. But also, was there anything in terms of our incentive structures or other systemic issues at the time that contributed to it? In other words, what did *we* do as a company to have brought the event on? It would have been easy enough to find out from the culprits themselves, had it not been for the hostile legal process recommended by our lawyer, and the immediate contraction on both sides that it brought. I'm not suggesting here that the instinct of defending the company was wrong. However, there are many different ways of defending a company, some of them smarter than others. As it played out, employing the lawyer cost us fifteen thousand pounds, and close to six months' worth of stress (as the other party, triggered by the formal proceedings we introduced, figured out multiple ways to make the case painful and complex, which cost us more legal fees and time). In the end, we didn't even file a lawsuit since – as is the case in nearly all such instances – the other party would have likely declared bankruptcy, while the legal costs on us mounted. All, or nearly all, of this to avoid staying in the discomfort of a very painful face-to-face conversation without third parties involved. This remains the biggest heartbreak, and one of the biggest lessons, of my career.

I'm quite convinced that I'm getting better, both in my professional and personal lives, at staying in a place that hurts. My capacity to be with fear, pain, doubt, disillusionment and regret is most definitely higher than it used to be. But while it continues to expand, I'm also aware of "survivor legacy", inherited from my grandma, which would have me believe that enduring pain and difficulty makes me more worthy. This is where I need to keep myself in check for my feminine leadership (expressed in not turning away from adversity) not to become seriously distorted.

My grandmother, a truly fabulous woman, the root of the tree of my closest family, had the most incredible stories to tell. Born in 1920 in Lviv in today's Ukraine (but part of the Polish territory at the time), she was raised and educated like a princess. At the age of 19, just as she passed her school finishing exam and was about to commence a law degree, in September of 1939 she lost virtually everything, as her entire world collapsed in front of her. Her mother fell ill and died while her father and brother emigrated to Hungary, leaving her behind, at the mercy of friends. As part of Polish intelligentsia, she was sought after by the Bolsheviks to be taken to one of the camps in Siberia and exterminated. Trying to escape those who were hunting her, in deep terror she knocked on doors of different friends of hers, often to be told, "I'm sorry but they have already been here to ask about you, you can't stay with us." On one occasion, she hid in a big bread oven that belonged to her friend's family of bakers. White fat worms crawled all over her in the darkness (amongst all the stories she told me, somehow this image stayed imprinted on my memory with most clarity) whenever there was a knock on the front door. Up till her nineties, she would wake up in the middle of the night, shivering, and sit up in her bed needing to tell herself the war was over. The essay I wrote, an interview with Joanna Polanowska, finished with the sentence she said looking me straight in the eye: "The most important thing is that we have survived."

I remember the first time I realised the impact of her legacy on my life, and how a part of me was in a way still living her, and her generation's, story. It was during a hypnosis session in London, after one of the waves of depression hit me hard again. When in a relaxed state I saw her face, clearly, and understood not in my mind but at a level of sensation in my body, that over my whole young life I've aspired to be her. The brave survivor. The one worthy of life and love because of the atrocities they'd been through. "My old age is made of silk," she used to say, which is an old Polish idiom expressing the preciousness of something. Young folks wouldn't say this anymore, just as young folks in my family no longer remember Grandma's stories. As I saw her face in a hypnotic vision, I realised I was living the life of an independent, super ambitious woman in business she might have wanted, but couldn't have (but was more than equipped to, with her qualities and talents). What also rose to the surface of my perception was the subconscious habit to seek my worthiness through surviving crisis, as an extension of her and a tribute to her.

I sense that many of us (perhaps you too) feel this burden – to live the calm, prosperous, somewhat uneventful (but secure!) lives our parents and grandparents couldn't have lived, and so did all they could to create the right set-up for us. By doing this, in their world, they gave us the most generous gift possible. And so, understandably, they feel truly upset when we are "wasting" it. But those are not the lives that we, the in-betweeners, during a global shift from one paradigm to another, are called to live. During this time of transition the ability to consciously live on the edge and to stay with discomfort – as long as not a habit borrowed from past generations – is essential.

# Letting The Punter Within Do His Thing

I have always enjoyed drag king acts, where an individual identifying as a female embraces and showcases her inner man. There tends to be quite a bit more drag queen than drag king acts on the cabaret scene and so there is something special about the latter for me. It's really satisfying to see women who are able to hone in on their inner masculine characters and proudly put them on display for the world to admire. They prove there's definitely a place for cleverly framed masculinity even in glamorous burlesque shows dominated by female characters. From all the drag king acts I've seen, I remember a particularly funny one featuring a disgruntled beefeater and also one performed by a woman with Down's syndrome who showcased a character referencing James Bond. They stood out because of their strong, unapologetic characters, created with a pinch of self-irony.

Even though this work is about the feminine rising, and maybe precisely because it is, I'd like to talk more about the inner masculine, particularly in the context of starting and running businesses. From what I sense and see around me and within me, we tend to belittle – or even emasculate – our inner men. We do it in two ways: either we distort their truth and get on the treadmill of performance at all costs to run away from inner discomfort (like I used to), or we silence them completely. I see the former tendency more – but not exclusively – amongst my business contacts and startup folk. I see the latter more within the more spiritual groups of friends I have, those who care more about pursuing their truth than mastering the material and pragmatic reality of life. Sadly, it often means that while they have an enormous potential to create things in the world, not much actually gets done, as they jump from one vision to another.

For people in both groups, it's surprisingly difficult to let the man within simply do his work – both internally, and as a consequence, in the world outside. It's not easy to trust that the inner man, not his distorted version but him in his essence, will be able to provide for you and perhaps for others in your life. Or that he will find a way of existing in the world without being pushed around by other parts of you such as the distorted (or manipulative) feminine, the traumatised child, or the shadow. When I meet people whose inner masculine part is shining and at ease, be it a woman or a man, I relax. I feel trust and a sense of things being right in the world when in connection with them. I can sense they are completely aligned with their truth and so it's easier for me to be completely aligned with mine.

Amongst women and men who exhibit strong masculine (or yang) leadership, decisions get made and things get done. There's objective progress because they find it fulfilling and like to understand, in tangible terms, how well they are doing. It's obvious what's important to them and that they are willing to stand by it. In so many ways, things are simple and straightforward. My dad has a strong masculine essence and so does my co-founder, and the current female CEO of my business. It's a pleasure to be around them when the situation demands that someone takes a stand. Our masculine part is driven, focused and competitive but not for the sake of proving something to anyone else. More because it's fun to make things happen, it makes our inner man feel alive. And there's nothing like resting by the fire, well-earned beer in hand, when a good chunk of work has been done. These days, GrantTree, run by our new CEO Nicky (who started five years ago as a client manager, then became a financial controller, a financial director, and penultimately managed one of our business units), can function without my and Daniel's involvement. We are truly blessed, as it's the dream a lot of entrepreneurs, even those aspiring to create self-managing teams and companies, never get to realise.

Importantly, by saying all this I don't want to imply that

feminine (or yin) leadership qualities, both within women and men, are less important or even less tangible. A woman or a man with a strong feminine aspect can be an inspiring leader, depending on the type of organisation they are in or challenges they find themselves facing. Still, in my view, people best equipped to handle a whole spectrum of trials in the modern world (and workplace) are those with both energies present and available to be brought into a given situation, depending on context. I also don't feel that feminine leadership qualities are particularly "natural" to women, while masculine are typically found in men. As tantric master Diana Richardson points out, while the female aspect is receptive, and the male aspect is active, we are all half women and half men anyway. It's the pressure of society to fulfil gender expectations that makes us fall into a gender stereotype. And it's not stereotypes that I'm concerned with in this work but two disparate sets of qualities of leadership that are found in people of all genders.

Amongst those with a strong masculine element and a sense of mission, great things get accomplished. Cathedrals and motorways between cities get built. Problems of all kinds get solved. Those who are vulnerable and too young or too old to fight the battles of life, are protected, kept safe. And if there's a crisis, there's a plan. Always. There's also a healthy sense of what's enough, when it's time to rest and recharge, in the nourishing shade of the feminine.

How to bring the inner masculine leadership centre to your job or your project? First of all, explicitly invite your inner man to take his throne. Secondly, don't judge his advice or decisions. They're likely to be pragmatic and focused on finding a solution to the problem at hand, so may not get you exactly what you've dreamt of. If you're disappointed by his guidance, it's quite possible you're not seeing that what is necessary for the time being is to get grounded in the reality of the material world, before you can implement your longer-term visions. Unless you are grounded, comfortable and feel safe as a person, your visions won't be sustainable anyway. Importantly, value your inner man for his contribution to your life and being in general. Thank him whenever you see a reason to. Compliment him on a job well done. And don't forget that he will only be truly fulfilled when he is of service to your inner feminine, which stands for love and well-being of all that exists, in its essence. But the feminine must support him, nourish him and let him rest. So that when he wakes up with sunrise the following day, he is ready for the fight with all that stands in the way of the change he wants to see in the world.

# Letting The Goddess Within Make Love

I saw plenty of amazing acts whilst an active burlesque artist. One I'll never forget was performed by a friend of mine, Violet Blaze, who impersonated Matron "Mama" Morton, the big lady prison guard from the musical Chicago (played by Queen Latifah in Chicago the movie). Violet was black, curvy and owned every little bit of her stage charisma. She was simply spilling her Goddess energy all over the admiring punters, from the moment she arrived on stage, dressed in electric violet (of course!) with more sparkly bits and sequins than you can possibly imagine. She fed her violet feather boa between her thighs and shook her boobies to demonstrate, as the lyrics of the song went, that "when you're good to Mama, Mama's good to you". She was so unashamedly and delightfully herself that all the women watching suddenly felt more electric in their own bodies and more aware of their own light. She was so damn sexy in her bombastic expression, all the men in the audience felt a little bit more alive. I remember Violet Blaze and her act when I doubt the Goddess within me. It helps.

As scientist, storyteller and TED speaker Brené Brown put it, it indeed is a courageous statement to rest and play in a world where constant busy-ness is a status symbol. A lot of businesspeople and startup founders I know live in cages of their own making. It's their fear of being anything else other than practical, goal-oriented, hyper-competitive, their well-ingrained habit of never showing any cracks in their appearance, emotionally or otherwise, that puts them there. I spent many years in a similar straitjacket of my own making. I didn't believe it was entirely up to me to choose how I show up in the world.

Based on my own experience of working with the masculine/feminine polarity within, as well as the wisdom of a variety of authors, some of which I quote on these pages, inviting your inner feminine to show up means you choose to trust the world that it can and will receive you in your softer place. It's way more interesting and multifaceted than "loosening up" but even that can be a good start. The feminine holds your creativity and vulnerability, your free expression and your playfulness (think Violet Blaze on stage!). On a deeper level, it points to your sense of ethics and values such as gratefulness, kindness, generosity, patience and resilience. In one word, love.

In consequence, to put it bluntly, unless you invest time into getting to know your inner woman, your inner man is impotent, from the point of view of meaningful impact on the world and on your own life. If the inner woman isn't integrated, he will continue acting and thrusting forward, without a meaningful aim, just for the sake of being active. It's the feminine aspect within you that gives the masculine his true purpose, the "why" behind the activity. I used to be afraid my inner woman would somewhat limit my inner man or clip his wings. Instead, when my feminine part is active, the plans, dreams and actions of my masculine part get taken to a different level. There's a renewed sense of what really matters, plus a sprinkle of a unique expression, joy, creative madness. On the other hand, the gift my inner woman receives from my inner man is that of getting grounded in the reality of what the world needs and how her gifts can be best seen and used. When the two parts are united everything comes together in wholeness. Several of my friends, both female and male, went through the process of awakening the inner woman and it was incredible to observe how their energy and way of being changed as a result. From my experience, it's not as much about softening, as it is about opening to life, opening to different dimensions of oneself. With this often comes, as it did for me, greater humility towards all aspects of life, a love affair with the great mystery we are all part of.

And a touch of playfulness and tongue-in-cheek attitude to oneself at the same time, à la Violet Blaze playing Matron "Mama" Morton.

# Your Inner Child At Work

While it may seem that strippers and children don't tend to hang out together, every mindful showgirl knows well that the true source of her creativity is the little one inside. This is why the more time and energy we invest into nourishing our inner children (and healing their wounds), the more we can expect for our creative brilliance to shine. A healthy inner child is an endless source of playfulness, fun and originality in our lives and in our creations. As Picasso famously pointed out, every child is an artist. As Ursula Le Guin said, a creative adult is a child who survived. As we grow up, we never really lose that inner artist but quite often (and sadly) we forget how to access them.

It's possible that you recognise your inner child as the one who continues throwing tantrums inside of you at least appropriate moments, as opposed to an endless source of joy and creativity. I certainly recognise this frustration from my own experience. I recently spent a few days with my family in Poland, where I grew up, and my inner child decided to act out. It reminded me loud and clear about all the times it didn't feel heard back when I was little, and that it still lives inside of me and, sometimes, feels terrified. The adult in me sweated a hell of a lot trying to calm the little girl down, finally to decide there's nothing to do but to witness the child go through everything it needs to go through, with as much compassion as possible.

This episode got me thinking, is there a place for my inner girl in the office? Is she welcome there at all? For a long time she hasn't been, just like in many other workplaces, possibly yours as well, as I believed this was no place for her. But she's always been my most sensitive inner radar, a radar tuned into how much fun and creativity there is in what I'm doing. Is my soul aligned with how I spend my time and where my energy goes?

Is a decision I've taken (and the way it will impact others) fair in the world of adults and how things tend to be done, or *really* fair, fair on a level of childlike innocence? Nobody else was able to answer these questions as precisely as she was, even if I wasn't always prepared to listen to her voice. It's because of her that I learnt to be biased towards generosity, for example encouraging people to take time off to heal emotionally after a difficult event in their lives, as opposed to focusing only on what impact their absence might have on the company.

Does your inner child get to speak, and be heard, when she or he is tired, threatened or simply bored? It doesn't have to mean their wishes will always be followed but she (or he) can be invited to share these longings, and the rest of you can make an effort to hear her out. Do appreciate how valuable a radar she is for when things appear to be fine but aren't, underneath the surface of things. She raises your attention to all that an adult might gloss over, and increases your sensitivity, sometimes unbearably so. She also finds something to laugh about in the most serious of situations. You might notice that the more grave something appears, often the easier it is for her to tune into playful lightness. Sometimes it takes a serendipitous event or a turn of a situation for her to step in.

My sister and I got really upset at each other recently. Having been very close as children, we've not been close as adults. We live in different countries and our life paths and careers took us in separate directions. I used to have expectations with regards to the nature of our friendship as adults, a while ago, which weren't workable for her. Then she had expectations around how I should show up when we spend time together, which I failed to meet. When we got together with our parents recently something in her exploded. Resentment felt pretty hard for both of us to contain. I got defensive, she got defensive. We really wanted to meet and yet there was little space in our interaction for anything beyond bitterness and trying to justify our own point of view. We parted without a customary hug as it didn't feel authentic to me in that moment. As she walked away I realised that millions of family members who don't talk to each other probably start off this way. There's a difficult conversation, too difficult for one or both sides to contain without showing resentment or getting defensive, despite their best efforts. Then somebody refuses a hug. Then people simply don't get in touch with each other because it feels unnecessary and why the hell should *I* apologise or show vulnerability anyway?! Months turn into years and the silence has nothing to do with the original incident, now surrounded by several layers of awkwardness. It's difficult to find anything to say anyway, after all this time. There's nothing one could say that comes with ease.

As I pondered this, in the desk drawer of my student-days bedroom at my parents' house I found a note my sister left for me about 15 years ago, when we still lived together in this house, with her bedroom next door, before I left for the UK. We used to pretend we were boys and write to each other in an elaborate language with quite a lot of code words and phrases that would seem like nonsense to an outsider. This note was written by a lad called Ruppert to a character called Stanislav. Ruppert was leaving for a summer scouts camp early in the morning and had a few things to say to Stan who was fast asleep at the time. I roared with laughter and cried a little as I read all this, scribbled in my sister's teenage handwriting. It hurt immensely to realise how far apart we've come since then. A little while later, an idea emerged: let's write back! Let's write back as Stan, who has received the letter all these years later but remains firmly rooted in his Stan self, as a friend and partner in crime of Ruppert's. The little girl clapped her hands and whirled around within me. Then the adult chipped in: absolutely NOT. We're in a different reality, a reality of conflict, pain and tragically-unmet expectations which may lead to a parting forever. To hell with childlike games that have no bearing on the present reality.

The little girl won. Stanislav wrote his letter, in response to all the things Ruppert mentioned all these years ago. I knew in that moment those characters were just as real (or unreal) and just as present as my sister's and my adult selves. Both handwritten letters were photographed and whatsapped. The awkwardness, which could have taken over for months or years, was now broken. The reality of pain and brokenness was just as present as the reality of a silly friendship. Or, maybe, what was real in the past and what is real now became two sides of the same coin. And what's the coin itself? That's subject to interpretation. A gift. A burden. Something that makes your life richer. Something to cherish. A nuisance. Something to lose or to throw away. Something to find.

# For The Love Of The Punter

Say what you will, but a showgirl without a punter is like the sun with nothing to shine its brilliance on. After all, what's the point of teasing with no one to tease? In my time, I've interacted with more and less keen and enthusiastic audiences, but still, every time I performed I was aware that my act is only as good as the degree to which it can attract and entertain others. And I was always delighted to receive good feedback on my stage presence, the storyline of my acts, costumes and gags. The best performers always have a way of interacting with their audience, creating an intimate relationship with it for the duration of the performance. Every time I was truly satisfied with my stage time, I felt an energetic thread connecting me with the punters. They gave me their keen attention, I gave them the best of my charisma as an entertainer; it felt like a palpable and intense cycle of energy. Their appreciation fed me, my expression fed them. With their interest they created my stardom.

I feel compelled to stop by and talk about the power of the healthy masculine. Without my dad and the qualities he brings, my close family would probably be messy and chaotic in ways that bring more suffering than joy. Without my inner man Bob, I would be lost, both as a professional and an individual. In the infinite complexity of things, the masculine discerns the simple way, the way that's possible to go, at this moment. Sometimes, in the middle of a business crisis or in relating with family, for example, it feels like there are a million possible routes to take, each leading to a trap. Some traps are hidden (but you can just about sense that they are there), some pretty obvious. I expect that you recognise this situation from your own experience. When all the roads seem to lead nowhere, it's easy to revert back to a way of doing things you know you've outgrown. And then, provided there is enough room, the masculine within you steps in. He discerns a way to go which may not seem very sophisticated but it works, or works for now. So simple that perhaps it crossed your mind before but you dismissed it as lame or not 111% aligned with the elusive (but surely sophisticated!) voice of your soul. But that is the path of least harm, and it's good enough for now.

The essence (as opposed to the distortion) of the masculine is a blessing. And when we don't acknowledge it, we spin endlessly in the bleak chaos (or, if you prefer, the endless complexity) of the universe. The inner man cuts through the Gordian Knot when it's time to, just like Alexander the Great did, instead of tediously untying it with his fingers, as the legend goes. And moves on to something else, something that's more within his sphere of influence to change, or at least to impact positively. There's an elegance and precision to the movements of his sword, particularly when directed from the place by deep care and love. And then, the focus swiftly shifts to something else that demands his service.

You might recognise your inner masculine as a place of stability and a place of ease. Everything may be spinning around you, and that's okay. It doesn't have anything to do with who he is in his centre. With ageless understanding and a sense of detachment he moves from one conflict to another, from a business crisis in one area to two or three in another he completely didn't expect. Praise be to his dedication, his commitment and his skill.

It's the mother that nurtures the child when it's smallest and at its most vulnerable, and makes him or her feel safe. It only makes sense as the smell, feel and voice of the mother are the only things the baby can recognise. Everything else, at the very beginning at least, seems totally unfamiliar and potentially threatening. However, it's the energy of the father that at some point prepares the child for initiation into adulthood. Shows her or him how to navigate life outside of the space of nourishing safety. Our inner masculine continues to play this role with regards to our inner child, if we let him, of course. His love isn't always tender like a mother's love and can feel challenging. But it's precisely the kind of love that we need in order to stand firmly rooted in our centre, amongst the chaos of the world around us.

# For The Appreciation Of Fear

There are no great artists that don't experience fear, at least from time to time. It could be the anxiety connected to how a new act will land with the punters. It could be the crowd not being particularly friendly and forgiving that night, or perhaps not sufficiently warmed up yet by other good acts. The other side of fear is full expression and great performers of all kinds know how to "ride" that fear and use it to their advantage. I remember being particularly nervous in front of a Canadian audience. It was the first time I was to perform abroad, let alone on a different continent, and I was worried. Would they understand me despite my remnants of an Eastern European accent? Would they appreciate my crazy acts that were more on the neo-burlesque path rather than the more traditional, glamorous burlesque side of things? As it turned out, the doubts weren't justified but a bit of stage fright helped me deliver a great performance.

In other words, if you, like me, experience fear or paralysis quite often, take it as a good sign. If you acknowledge and embrace it, you are already on the path of transformation. As Jane Roberts, psychic and spiritual medium, mentions in *The Nature of Personal Reality*, what we deny in any part of our being divorces us from the entirety of who are. This compels me to lean in to fear. Both the fear each of us faces in times of individual transition – which I know so well – and the collective fear, which can be impossible to separate from a process of collective transformation. Fear tends to be difficult to stay with and work with as it breeds more fear. Essentially though, it's simply part of the process of change. Often, a portal through which a new vision for a possible reality comes in.

And so, I encourage you to work on creating more compassion for your own fear. A part of this, you might discover, is how it links to the collective fear which also wants to be acknowledged, or held. Everything that holds us back is already part of the change of mentality that's occurring. And because of this it needs to be seen and heard. In a way, fear is – and historically has always been – the resistance against a new movement or form of leadership emerging. The feminine way of dealing with resistance is to soften into it. Or, to allow and investigate it. I like psychologist Tara Brach's approach to dealing with difficult feelings and I often use the RAIN meditation from her toolkit. RAIN stands for recognise, allow, investigate and nurture. I find that the investigation stage is typically the most challenging one and takes me the most time to go through properly. When I plunge deeper into the fear, my face cringes and my body wants to contract. But it's only when I have a deeper connection with my fear that I can ask what it needs and how best to be with it.

So, instead of striving to push your fear away, simply sit with it, allow it the space it needs so transformation can happen. And as you become more deeply familiar with your own fear, it's impossible to be a harsh judge of fears present in the collective space. They are simply the necessary conduit for progress. And so, as long as collective fear doesn't become a collective paralysis, it's a rich, fertile ground to explore, for example in an artistic way. Befriend your fear as an inevitable sign of a breakthrough coming.

# How To Be C.U.N.T.

I would like to bring a new meaning to the word "cunt".

On one hand, it is possibly the most offensive word in the English language. On the other, it's a word with a lot of power and an extremely rich etymology. To be C.U.N.T. is, to me, to have achieved a certain level of mastery when it comes to balancing your inner feminine and masculine energies, and to have extended that to your business, your work, or whatever creative effort is important to you.

I chose the word "cunt" because of its unapologetic, primal – even though accursed – energy. Cunt vibrates power and solidity with a twinge of dark energy. You do not say "cunt" lightly. Even if you mean to, it comes out heavy. It doesn't slip off the tongue but drops out of your mouth heavy like a rock, a dark seed now planted in your neighbour's garden at night, not easy to retrieve. Collectively, we've chosen this word to encompass our distrust of the feminine essence and potency over many centuries. It's time to create a different narrative.

As the Bible says, "In the beginning was the Word" (John 1:1). In the context of reclaiming leadership from the feminine aspect, this word could well be "cunt". I choose to reclaim it in my own language as an expression of appreciation for my feminine essence. Not only in its gentle form but particularly in its dark, potent, vast and unexplored quality. Tantric masters refer to cunt (or yoni) as the only temple in this universe that conceives, and births, life. I hope it can become a temple of life for the movement of the empowered feminine rising, in partnership with, and supported by, the empowered masculine.

I'm usually careful about simplifying things but simplifications are sometimes useful in getting a message across and also make it easier to grasp and implement it. And so, I allowed for my masculine to make a decision here and create a simplification which some of you may find helpful to take away something tangible from this book (and my masculine part, I like to refer to as Bob, loves tangible shit).

## C.U.N.T.s Are Curious, Unapologetic, Notorious And Trustful.

Being curious and trustful are quintessentially feminine attributes which surround – or hold space for – the notoriety and unapologetic nature of the essence of the masculine.

You probably know someone who is curious and trustful by nature but not much can be said about their ability to drive and manifest things in the world. I can easily picture someone with these characteristics; I can both see them shine and also see them feeling deeply disappointed or betrayed by reality. Not because they are "too good for this world", more because they haven't taken the necessary steps to claim their own life, and their dreams with it. I've met a lot of visionaries or "wantrepreneurs" of the type and I'm sure you have too. I used to be one also, many years ago, bumping into startup founders at meetups and wishing one day I'd be one of them. When an opportunity presented itself, I invited the masculine within me to act, I gave him space to do what he needed to do to make tangible things happen, with buckets of resilience and willpower. And with his continuous support I achieved more in the startup space than I ever thought I was capable of.

If you have boundless creativity but tend to feel stuck moving your projects forward, check where your inner man currently resides. Does he have a firm seat within you, taking part in decision making and driving the action, or has he been pushed away, perhaps, to the peripheries of your being? Can you feel him ready to commit to a particular direction and take actions necessary to accomplish goals you've set for yourself? Remember that you can call on his support at any moment, particularly if you need more clarity, on a practical level, around pursuing your purpose.

On the other end of the spectrum, you can easily imagine someone who is unapologetic and notorious but not very trustful and open to life or to other people. They definitely get things done aplenty, possibly anything they want gets manifested sooner or later. Some are in awe watching them work. But sooner or later they crash spiritually and start questioning: why do anything anymore? What's the point of doing what you do? Particularly once bills are paid, holidays have been had, stuff that you wanted to have is more or less all affordable and suddenly loses its appeal. And what's the point of buying what you can easily afford?

I remember when my husband and I were looking for a place to buy, on a mortgage, with a deposit well earned by our entrepreneurial blood, sweat and tears, ready in our bank account. Interestingly, we were most drawn to places that were slightly beyond what was achievable financially. In the end we settled for a cost-effective option but in a great location, leaving us with a budget to do a complete refurbishment of the place, buy some furniture, order funky wall art and not be broke afterwards. I thank heavens to this day that that's the choice that we made. Would we have been happier in one of the expensive places? Definitely not. A highly ambitious, purely unapologetic and notorious person might decide differently in such circumstances though, just to give themselves something to strive for, a new stretch goal. But at some point the inevitable crash will come, as striving without a meaningful purpose is unsustainable. In other words, one could dedicate a lot of effort to climbing the metaphorical ladder, only to find out, sometimes years or decades later, that it was leaning against the wrong tree. I'm not trying to diminish the value of setting financial goals and investing in whatever you desire upon achieving them. I'm simply advocating, based on personal experience, being more in tune with why you want the things you want and if having them is likely to actually add to your happiness levels.

# C.U.N.T. Explained

What is curiosity? For me, it's a quality of fundamental openness to life. Where does the energy want to flow, in this situation, or in the context of this particular relationship?

In my perception this has everything to do with how connected I am, first to myself, my own needs, desires, boundaries and beliefs; then with other people in a given situation; then with the bigger picture of a relationship, outside of the immediacy of what's happening right now.

Curiosity means staying in openness and flow between these three levels. This means you easily move from one to another and back. It doesn't mean, however, that I'm always open to everything that comes; contractions and boundaries are natural. But I can stay in connection with my own contraction while remaining in curiosity or openness to a situation. Being curious is to be free, unbounded, unrestricted. Without sufficient curiosity we inevitably get stuck – in our perspective, in our story, in the way we choose to interpret the world.

We try to squash the truth of a situation, which is infinitely complex and fascinating, into the box of our perception. And, if we manage to do that, we inevitably feel disappointed, sooner or later, that's all there is to reality.

Being unapologetic also feels like being utterly free to me, on a level of my expression in the world. I am not bound by convention or by external norms. I can choose to abide by them, of course, but it's a free and conscious choice. I am not bound by my own shame and sense of not being enough or not belonging in the world. Those feelings may come but they don't have any power over me. I also don't have to prove that I am worthy or strive to look good in front of anyone. I know that I deeply deserve life in its fullest expression, including my unique imprint. And from the place of this knowing, I act.

A truly unapologetic person isn't a show-off but remains innocent, pure and joyful like a child. In other words, she or he isn't tainted by cynicism, disbelief, resentment or fear. Everything an unapologetic person does, they do in the light, in full view, for there is nothing to hide.

Notoriety, not in the ill-fame sense of the word but more a badass relentlessness, is a domain of entrepreneurs with a strong masculine leadership. It reminds me of what Paul Graham, famous entrepreneur, computer scientist and venture capitalist refers to as "being an animal"; he chooses entrepreneurs with this quality (amongst others) to join Y Combinator, possibly the most famous incubator globally he created. He works with those who impose their dream on the world with relentlessness that knows no hesitation, until the world has no choice but to accommodate your dream and shape itself around it, to reference Tony Hsieh, founder of Zappos.

Yes, some people will get rubbed up the wrong way. But, as my friend puts it, there's no way to be a real entrepreneur and not to piss someone off along the way. And preferably an entire industry which is stuck in its ways and thoroughly ready for disruption.

To me being notorious also implies being relentless about improving oneself. It means constantly reinventing oneself, shedding skins, to find an iteration of an idea, belief or behaviour that works in the business context. To be notorious is to be perpetual and unstoppable even when things don't look pretty or promising, like the wheel of fortune. It's to be truly committed. I don't see a lot of unwavering commitment in the world – and also in myself – these days. We move from one thing to another in the hope of feeling more comfortable, more recognised, more special. And yet we come across a set of largely similar issues everywhere we go. Obviously, we take these issues there ourselves.

Being trustful is a beautiful quality of the feminine aspect which rounds up the feminine-masculine balance of an entrepreneur of the future. Trust is possibly the most complex quality to define, and has so many dimensions. When I ask an intelligent candidate I'm interviewing what trust means to them, I often get a reply I haven't even considered before. I remember how I felt when I first heard, in personal development circles, the phrase "trust the process". I was really frustrated. What the hell does this even mean? Which process, mine, someone else's, the process of the world at large? And what if those are at odds with one another?

These days I don't even try to answer these questions. I can, in most cases, drop into "trusting the process" without the need to know exactly where the boundaries of this process are, where it might be going, or what it all has to do with me.

It's possible that the idea of being trustful gives you the creeps. It's possible that you feel you've worked hard to carve out a little corner of the world where you feel safe and you don't intend to trust anyone or anything outside of that corner. I appreciate what you feel since I keep on discovering how, where it comes to my view of life, I have "made" some things safe, and other things risky or even untouchable.

The truth is, though, that we have to find ways to abandon the safety we've created in order to meet ourselves fully in a place where nothing is controllable. In a place where life flows.

It may be that you are considering working part-time (which is something that I have decided to do) and taking time for yourself, just to do whatever you please, or even nothing at all for a while, is a scary idea. Being a super-busy professional with a thriving career has become a status symbol, a new social norm to follow if you want to feel that you belong to the modern urban world. It could be a decision to do with relating, perhaps you're on the brink of committing to someone, whatever this means to you, or quite the opposite, a relationship you are in has become stale and needs to end. Maybe it's time to take the leap – in terms of time, energy, or cash – and pursue that project, or business, you've been dreaming about for a while.

Leaning into uncertainty doesn't mean jumping off the bridge of what you currently trust just for the sake of proving to yourself that you can. A few years ago, when we had transparent financials but no self-set salaries at GrantTree, my co-founder and I, shaking slightly in our boots, having read *Maverick!* by Ricardo Semler, decided to make that big move and give people individual responsibility for setting their pay. Today, we realise that at the time, we'd done nowhere near the amount of background work required for things not to blow up in our faces. People in the company didn't understand what commercial sustainability meant. We had next to no stats demonstrating what salaries companies of a similar size in our market paid, or what proportion of their revenue was spent on payroll. We'd tried to create a pay matrix based on models we'd found but it didn't resonate with most people. All sorts of pieces were not in place but we couldn't even see it at the time. But we were ambitious little motherf*ckers. And so we took the leap.

Our first employee decided to uplift his salary significantly, with not enough (in my opinion) market research to back his decision. I got scared as to what impact it would have on the wider team and how we could possibly sustain a significant increase across the board, and so I advised him against the decision. It may have been better to let it all play out, but potential damage to the company felt, at least to me, threatening. It all blew up eventually and, like dogs with tails between our legs, my co-founder and I took a decision to pull the self-set salary project back for now. A few years later, when we were in a much better position organisational awareness-wise, we implemented it again, with no major problems (though some people at GrantTree still dislike having the responsibility for setting their salary!).

What I've tried to say above is that – to be blunt – trustful doesn't equal stupid or blasé. A trustful person doesn't not get out of bed in the knowledge that the Universe will provide for them anyway. She or he jumps out of bed precisely to meet and receive all that's lined up for them already (but won't manifest fully if it's not noticed and appreciated). Trustful doesn't mean having the "whatever" attitude and not caring about the outcome. It has everything to do with being smart and considerate about things, precisely because you expect them to work out in the best way for you. To be trustful is to be held in safety because you've chosen – and decided to trust – yourself first. As the saying goes, trust in Allah, but don't forget to tie your camel. Only once you've done that can you fully let go.

# If I Ruled The World

As I begin to write this, what's on my mind are the opening lines of Harry Secombe's *If I Ruled the World*, as performed by one of my favourite jazz singers, Jamie Cullum, at the BBC Proms 2010. If you haven't heard this marvellous version of the jazz standard, you can easily find it on YouTube. As a performer you will experience moments when you feel literally on top of the world. It seems that the stars have aligned to help you be in the perfect place in the perfect moment, in front of a perfect audience. The performance flows effortlessly and perhaps, struck by inspiration, you add something – a joke, a dance move, a little interaction with the audience – that wasn't there before but really makes the act shine. During my best performances I recall feeling like I was having energetic sex with the audience. Their energy and attention fed me and because of it I was able to give more of myself back to them. Just like in a beautiful sexual experience, we gave energy, enthusiasm and love to each other, and received from each other.

The truth is, whether you are a performer or not, each one of us already and unequivocally rules our own world. Some of us find it harder to acknowledge, as it's easy to see what influence those more "powerful" than us, such as workplace bosses, landlords, politicians, etc have on our lives. However, there are just as many versions of reality as there are people. We are powerful beings, whether or not we choose to acknowledge it. Everything I do, preceded by what I say, preceded by what I think, rooted in what I've been shaped to – or chose to – believe, creates ripples on the endlessly stretching surface of the lake of possibility.

"Envision, create and believe in your own universe, and the universe will form around you," argues Tony Hsieh in *Delivering Happiness*. The little manifesto book talks about how his wildly successful e-commerce company, Zappos, not only came to be, but stayed true to its values and ideology, also thanks to adopting holacracy, all the way through to its acquisition by Amazon. I remembered his suggestion to "envision, create and believe in your own universe" for two reasons. Obviously because this resonates with me but also because – as per his memories in the book – Tony quite coolly used it to chat up an attractive girl who came to one of the raves he used to organise in pre-Zappos days. As he describes all the love that went into the endeavour, I imagine it's the feeling of rave-like unity created in his community of friends he later sought to reproduce in the business world.

Coming back to *If I Ruled the World* mentioned at the beginning of this chapter, "every voice would be a voice to be heard" is far from a cheesy line for me. Our deepest need, while in these bodies and on this planet, is to be heard (or seen, or touched, depending on how you tend to experience the world through your senses). What is your part to play in the run-up to the world of the future where every voice indeed is a voice worth hearing? When I sense into mine, creating and being part of organisations where sustainability and wholesomeness meet is definitely part of it. The way I currently act on this calling is to be part of a company I started over nine years ago where people respect one another, and are as a matter of principle trusted to do great work just because that's the way we're wired (instead of being bullied into performing).

At GrantTree, work isn't always bliss; we do have some tedious things to do every day (self-management, since there are no dedicated managers in the company, being one of those tedious things, for many people). But overall, I believe we've removed some – not all – barriers that stood in the way of us being able to do great work, which isn't driven primarily by fear of underperforming and losing your job. We have also added some considerable challenges that a lot of people never have to face in their work, as someone else makes decisions for them and tells them what to do – such as curating your own career, resolving conflicts with your colleagues, and calibrating the value of the work that you do, including both the commercial and not directly commercial elements of it. But we believe that a workplace which is challenging in this way brings us closer to the kind of future we can and want to live in, both in and out of the workplace. And a surprising amount of other founders and people who contribute to their companies do too.

On our journey we've been inspired by countless authors, founders and practitioners; the more we study the topic, the more fascinating people and materials we come across. If you'd like to see an (ever-expanding) list of references that have been helpful to us on this journey, see the resources section at the end of this book or visit https://danieltenner.com/open-cultures/.

# Epilogue: From Me To You, Message In A Bottle

I used to like sending out messages and burying treasures for someone to find accidentally someday, maybe. Some of them were of questionable quality – as part of a secret project when I was just a few years old, I recall filling a glass jar with different household chemicals and burying it carefully and with solemnity in the fields around my family's summer house. Back then I was intensely curious what could be achieved by mixing washing powder with washing-up liquid and my dad's shaving foam. Poor Earth. I also recall a walkabout theatre performance I took a part in as an adult where, after my monologue, I shared a bottle, with a message inside, with my small audience. Here's what comes now and wants to be committed to the ground.

*It's not easy to be human, particularly in a civilisation that could be coming to an end, because of the decisions we've made and the resources we've carelessly used up. And in this pain, there's also beauty. Or, perhaps, it simply sprouts from the same source where the pain is birthed. We know nothing. In the bigger spectrum of things, we can achieve nothing. Our weary eyes still stray to the horizon, though down this road we've been so many times, following the lyrics of my favourite Pink Floyd song. And yet, we're all part of the giant river of existence which flows through spacetime, and our individual actions matter. Our alignment matters and our happiness matters. In my experience, more happiness and alignment can be achieved in companies which, for the purposes of this book, I've called organisations of the future. These companies are created, led and developed by people who see themselves fully, strive to see and hear others and appreciate the value of work as a container to find their mastery, push their limits and create meaning for themselves.*

*And so, whoever you are, whatever you're up to in life, may you be happy, may you be free, may you (and your organisation or project) receive all the good things this life has to offer.*

# Acknowledgements

I've heard Robert Holden say, shoeless and in his brightly coloured socks, while on a Hay House workshop stage, that we never write alone. We write with past generations standing behind us and cheering us on, and with future generations welcoming already what's being created. I could feel this sometimes, in moments of doubt, and I'm grateful that as a writer, and as a being, I'm never disconnected. I'm grateful to all those who encouraged me to write, such as Rex Rafiq and for all the forces and guides that kept me going, through the highs and lows.

Pragmatically speaking, I'd like to thank everyone who works and has worked in the business that I started, GrantTree. I thank you because of your faith in what we're doing, despite moments of personal and collective doubt. I thank you because your professional excellence and sense of ownership of your work (which often astounds me) has enabled me to step away from day-to-day responsibilities in the business to find myself again – beyond the identity of an entrepreneur – and to write this book. I thank my first editor Stephanie Hale from Oxford Literary Consultancy, who helped me rethink and reshape the book and all those who encouraged me to keep going when the book was in its early stages, chiefly Anna Downey, founder of Buzzbar. I thank those who contributed feedback comments: Rob Fitzpatrick, my colleagues at GrantTree Marcin Gozdzik, Nicky Johnson, Rob Kellner, Al Valentini. Finally, I thank the team at John Hunt Publishing for support throughout the production and the publishing process.

I also thank my husband, one of the smartest and most beautiful people that I know, for insisting on not reading this book until it was in its final version, particularly since we've co-created so many things in the past. In this way, without his influence, I experienced the absolute freedom (and necessity) to find a voice which was entirely my own.

I thank Life Force for glowing in me and flowing through me to birth this work. I'm deeply grateful to be here – on this planet, and also in this current place in life, as a published author. I feel able and ready to spread my creative wings like never before and take off wherever I am guided to next.

# Bibliography And Recommended Reading

Bakke, Dennis. *Joy at Work: A Revolutionary Approach To Fun on the Job*, 2005

Beard, Mary. *Women & Power*, 2017

Blackie, Sharon. *If Women Rose Rooted: The Journey to Authenticity and Belonging*, 2016

Deida, David. *The Way Of The Superior Man*, 2004

Hsieh, Tony. *Delivering Happiness: A Path to Profits, Passion, and Purpose*, 2010

Jung, Carl. *"The Philosophical Tree"*, *Alchemical Studies*, 1945

Kegan, Robert and Laskow Lahey, Lisa, et al. *An Everyone Culture*, 2016

Kenyon, Tom and Sion, Judy. *The Magdalen Manuscript: The Alchemies of Horus & the Sex Magic of Isis*, 2002

Laloux, Frederic. *Reinventing Organisations*, 2014

Laskow Lahey, Lisa; Souvaine, Emily; Kegan, Robert; Goodman, Robert; Felix, Sally. *A Guide to the Subject-Object Interview: Its Administration and Interpretation*, 2011

Lushwala, Arkan. *The Time of the Black Jaguar: An Offering of Indigenous Wisdom for the Continuity of Life on Earth*, 2012

Lushwala, Arkan. *Deer and Thunder*, 2018

McGregor, Douglas. *The Human Side of Enterprise*, 1960

Pinkola Estés, Clarissa. *Women Who Run With The Wolves: Myths and Stories of the Wild Woman Archetype*, 2009

Richardson, Diana. *Tantric Orgasm for Women*, 2004

Richardson, Diana and Richardson, Michael. *Tantric Sex for Men: Making Love a Meditation*, 2010

Robertson, Brian. Holacracy: *The Revolutionary Management System that Abolishes Hierarchy*, 2016

Semler, Ricardo. *Maverick! The Success Story Behind the World's Most Unusual Workplace*, 2001

Ware, Bronnie. *Top Five Regrets of the Dying: A Life Transformed by the Dearly Departing*, 2019

BOOKS

# O-BOOKS

# SPIRITUALITY

O is a symbol of the world, of oneness and unity; this eye
represents knowledge and insight. We publish titles on general
spirituality and living a spiritual life. We aim to inform and help
you on your own journey in this life.
If you have enjoyed this book, why not tell other readers by
posting a review on your preferred book site?

## Recent bestsellers from O-Books are:

### Heart of Tantric Sex
Diana Richardson
Revealing Eastern secrets of deep love and intimacy to Western
couples.
Paperback: 978-1-90381-637-0 ebook: 978-1-84694-637-0

### Crystal Prescriptions
The A-Z guide to over 1,200 symptoms and their healing crystals
Judy Hall
The first in the popular series of eight books, this handy little
guide is packed as tight as a pill-bottle with crystal remedies for
ailments.
Paperback: 978-1-90504-740-6 ebook: 978-1-84694-629-5

## Your Simple Path
Find Happiness in every step
Ian Tucker
A guide to helping us reconnect with what is really important in
our lives.
Paperback: 978-1-78279-349-6 ebook: 978-1-78279-348-9

## 365 Days of Wisdom
Daily Messages To Inspire You Through The Year
Dadi Janki
Daily messages which cool the mind, warm the heart and guide
you along your journey.
Paperback: 978-1-84694-863-3 ebook: 978-1-84694-864-0

## Body of Wisdom
Women's Spiritual Power and How it Serves
Hilary Hart
Bringing together the dreams and experiences of women across
the world with today's most visionary spiritual teachers.
Paperback: 978-1-78099-696-7 ebook: 978-1-78099-695-0

## Dying to Be Free
From Enforced Secrecy to Near Death to True Transformation
Hannah Robinson
After an unexpected accident and near-death experience, Hannah
Robinson found herself radically transforming her life, while a
remarkable new insight altered her relationship with her father, a
practising Catholic priest.
Paperback: 978-1-78535-254-6 ebook: 978-1-78535-255-3

## The Ecology of the Soul
A Manual of Peace, Power and Personal Growth for Real People
in the Real World
Aidan Walker
Balance your own inner Ecology of the Soul to regain your
natural state of peace, power and wellbeing.
Paperback: 978-1-78279-850-7 ebook: 978-1-78279-849-1

## Not I, Not other than I
The Life and Teachings of Russel Williams
Steve Taylor, Russel Williams
The miraculous life and inspiring teachings of one of the World's
greatest living Sages.
Paperback: 978-1-78279-729-6 ebook: 978-1-78279-728-9

## On the Other Side of Love
A woman's unconventional journey towards wisdom
Muriel Maufroy
When life has lost all meaning, what do you do?
Paperback: 978-1-78535-281-2 ebook: 978-1-78535-282-9

## Practicing A Course In Miracles
A translation of the Workbook in plain language, with
mentor's notes
Elizabeth A. Cronkhite
The practical second and third volumes of The Plain-Language
*A Course In Miracles*.
Paperback: 978-1-84694-403-1 ebook: 978-1-78099-072-9

## Quantum Bliss
The Quantum Mechanics of Happiness, Abundance, and Health
George S. Mentz
*Quantum Bliss* is the breakthrough summary of success and
spirituality secrets that customers have been waiting for.
Paperback: 978-1-78535-203-4 ebook: 978-1-78535-204-1

## The Upside Down Mountain
Mags MacKean
A must-read for anyone weary of chasing success and happiness
– one woman's inspirational journey swapping the uphill slog for
the downhill slope.
Paperback: 978-1-78535-171-6 ebook: 978-1-78535-172-3

## Your Personal Tuning Fork
The Endocrine System
Deborah Bates
Discover your body's health secret, the endocrine system, and
'twang' your way to sustainable health!
Paperback: 978-1-84694-503-8 ebook: 978-1-78099-697-4

Readers of ebooks can buy or view any of these bestsellers by
clicking on the live link in the title. Most titles are published
in paperback and as an ebook. Paperbacks are available in
traditional bookshops. Both print and ebook formats are
available online.
Find more titles and sign up to our readers' newsletter at
http://www.johnhuntpublishing.com/mind-body-spirit
Follow us on Facebook at https://www.facebook.com/OBooks/
and Twitter at https://twitter.com/obooks